The Complete Greek Tragedies
Edited by David Grene and Richmond Lattimore

Euripides I

Alcestis
Translated by Richmond Lattimore

The Medea
Translated by Rex Warner

The Heracleidae
Translated by Ralph Gladstone

Hippolytus
Translated by David Grene

With an Introduction by Richmond Lattimore

WASHINGTON SQUARE PRESS
POCKET BOOKS • NEW YORK

The Complete Greek Tragedies

EURIPIDES I

University of Chicago Press edition published February, 1955

WASHINGTON SQUARE PRESS edition published July, 1967

4th printing.....................August, 1971

Acknowledgments

The Medea: From *Three Great Plays of Euripides,* Translated by Rex Warner. Reprinted by permission of The New American Library, Inc., and the Bodley Head, Ltd.

L

Published by
POCKET BOOKS, a division of Simon & Schuster, Inc.,
630 Fifth Avenue, New York, N.Y.

WASHINGTON SQUARE PRESS editions are distributed in the U.S. by Simon & Schuster, Inc., 630 Fifth Avenue, York, N.Y. 10020 and in Canada by Simon & Schuster of Canada, Ltd., Richmond Hill, Ontario, Canada.

Standard Book Number: 671–47807–9.

GENERAL INTRODUCTION

WE ARE told that Euripides, the son of Mnesarchus or Mnesarchides, was born at some time between 485 and 480 B.C., presented his first set of tragedies in 455, and won his first victory in 441, won only four victories during his lifetime, left Athens probably in 408 for the court of King Archelaus of Macedon, and died there late in 407 or early in 406. He wrote perhaps eighty-eight plays (twenty-two sets of four); nineteen survive under his name, though *Rhesus* may not be his.

Such seems to be the basic and believable vita (though I suspect that the dates for birth and first presentation are too early). We may ignore the fanciful gossip that passes for additional biography, but consider the critical opinions of the comic poets. The conclusion is that Euripides was only moderately successful in his own lifetime, though famous and influential after death. He won seldom but produced again and again. He was parodied and ridiculed by the comic poets more often and more brutally (and more intelligently, too) than any other literary man in Athens. This fact itself means that he made more of an impression than the now obscure competitors who must have beaten him again and again.

Plainly, he wrote shockers, and it is not enough to say that this was because he was an innovator. He was, but so were his predecessors. Aeschylus was more daring, drastic, and original; Sophocles was no serene and static classicist. Perhaps the most significant remark about Euripides and Sophocles is that supposed to have been made by Sophocles, that he himself showed men as they ought to be (or as one ought to show them) but Euripides showed them as they actually were. Whether or not Sophocles ever said this, it is true. Euripides was basically a realist, despite contrary tendencies toward fantasy and romance. The only materials available for his tragedies were the old heroic sagas. He used them as if they told the story not of characters heroic in all dimensions, but of real everyday people. From the high legends of Jason and Heracles he chose to enact the moments of the heroes' decay and disintegration. What, he asks, does it feel like to have your wife die for you, and what kind of man will let her do it? What does it feel like to have murdered your mother? His Admetus fights hard to deceive himself, but we all see that he is a coward; his Orestes is a bad mental case with fits and seizures. Creusa, brutally violated by Apollo and then robbed of the baby she had guiltily borne, does not dance decorously out of the story like Pindar's Evadne in similar circumstances; the shame sticks with her, as if she were a real girl with a real experience; and Apollo, while managing that all comes well in the end, hides behind his temple and lets his sister speak for him.

Though the judges of Dionysus disapproved, there cannot be much doubt that the audience was fascinated even when it was not pleased. Was this enough, though? The sense of defeat and disappointment is constantly there in Euripides. It makes him bring to the fore those who are weak or oppressed, the despised and misunderstood: women, children, slaves, captives, strangers, barbarians. Women as chief characters outnumber men, and most of his choruses are female. It is not that he is "for" them or "against" them; he merely tries to present action from their point of view, and they fascinate him. So do children, but here his realism fails: obviously, he knew little about them. His servants are true to life, while his heroes who deliver the oppressed are wooden.

Euripides is sometimes perhaps more pathetic than tragic. The hero (or heroine) in Sophocles is prepared to fight stubbornly to the last; his Teucer, alone against an army full of warriors who could beat him singlehanded, acts as if he were the champion with an army at his back. Many characters of Euripides spend all their time trying to run away from something. Ion and Hippolytus -are blissfully happy only while they lead do-nothing lives; then the real world with its entanglements catches up with them, and they are miserable. His choruses are not the first to long for the wings of the dove, but they do it oftenest; in him the drive to escape becomes an insistent, recurrent motive. Even his own invention, bright optimistic romantic comedy, becomes drama of escape. Usually, escape is impossible. He believed in a world he disliked. His gods represent this world.

With Euripides, tragedy is either transcending itself or going into a decline, in any case turning into something else. If Euripides is less of a master in his own medium than Aeschylus and Sophocles, it is partly because he was less happy in that medium. This shows in faults which his greatest admirers will concede. His pathos may degenerate into sentimentality. There are signs of haste, slovenliness, inconsequence, windiness, in most of his best plays. Some whole plays are mediocre. His most characteristic fault is to try to get too much into a single plot or character or situation. His Medea is several kinds of woman unsuccessfully assembled; his *Andromache* has two badly connected plots. He wrote some lovely lyrics, but often (as in *Helen*) they have nothing to do with what is going on in the play. And so on. His faults are obvious. Equally obvious is his genius. He is the father of the romantic comedy, the problem play. He has given us a series of unforgettable characters. There has never been anyone else like him.

RICHMOND LATTIMORE

BRYN MAWR COLLEGE

CONTENTS

ALCESTIS

Translated by Richmond Lattimore

INTRODUCTION TO *ALCESTIS*

The Legend

THE origins of the story as it is told by Euripides are difficult to trace. We hear of Admetus and of Alcestis, "loveliest of all the daughters of Pelias," in the *Iliad*, but only as parents of Eumelus, one of the Achaeans at Troy. There is an allusion to the story as Euripides tells it in the *skolion* or drinking catch attributed to the little-known poetess Praxilla:

> Mark the saying of Admetus, dear friend, and make
> friends with the brave.
> Keep away from cowards, knowing that there is little
> grace in them.

We also know that Phrynichus, a dramatic poet of the early fifth century, used what seems to have been essentially the same version as that which Euripides followed. The best conclusion, though it is tentative, is that Euripides did not add any "facts" to the legend as he received it. The originality of the play would rather lie in the way in which he approached a known, though not particularly well-known, story from a new angle and with a new emphasis.

The Play

Grant, then, the basic outline of the plot: Alcestis voluntarily dying for her husband when his father and mother would not; Alcestis and Admetus delivered by Admetus' true friend, Heracles, who is guided by the remote hand of Apollo, also a true friend of Admetus. One may emphasize the heroism of Alcestis and the staunchness of Heracles, as against the way in which mother and father fail wretchedly in the crisis. This is as far as our *skolion* goes, for whether or not "the brave" designates both Alcestis and Heracles or only one, "cowards" means the mother and father, not Admetus himself. Admetus is merely the subject about whom these operations, of dying or refusing to die, revolve; his own character does not come into question.

Euripides took a different kind of interest. He gives Alcestis full honors. The beginning of the play is all hers, and she is the center of all memories throughout the play. If she appears cold and self-righteous, if she reserves her passion, on stage, for her children, and talks only business with Admetus, this is rather the embarrassment of being disappointed in him than coldness. Endearments addressed to Admetus at this time would be intolerable. Her true nature is brought out by what servants and others have to say about her. Pheres, the father, is effectively dealt with in his one scene. It is true he wins his argument, but all the justification in the world does not save him from being a horrible old man. But the principal character is Admetus. The theme of the drama is not "if a wife dies for her husband, how brave and devoted the wife," so much as "if a husband lets his wife die for him, what manner of man must that husband be?"

Admetus is drawn to the life, without mercy. He has all the superficial graces and sincerely loves his wife and children, but he lacks the courage to die as he ought instead of letting his wife die for him; and, further, he lacks the courage to admit, to himself or anyone else, that he ought to be dying but dare not do it. He has, however, one solid virtue. For if he and Alcestis are at last saved not by his own strength and resolution but by Heracles under authority of Apollo, yet there is good reason why these august persons should be so devoted to him. Admetus is the best of friends. The right treatment of guests is a passion, almost an obsession, with him, and in this matter his conviction makes him firm enough to override so great a man as Heracles, with a show of force quite different from his ungrounded violence against Pheres. We may call him hospitable. But if we do, we must understand that, while the lavish entertainment of visitors was a special tradition in Thessaly, the hospitality of Admetus goes far beyond this and is no merely sociable virtue. Rather, this is the old Homeric *xenia*. It is one of the steps by which society progresses from savagery to civilization, when strangers make a willing, immediate, and permanent agreement to be friends. In this sense, *xenia* also includes cases at least of the nonabuse of power against those over whom one has power. Apollo, for punishment, was put at the mercy of Admetus, and Admetus gave him fair and friendly treatment (ll. 8–10; 222–24; 568–79). A different king might have reveled in his power over such a subject and acted outrageously. This is what Laomedon, king of Troy, did to Apollo and Poseidon (*Iliad* xxi. 441–60), and Poseidon never forgave him or his people. So, too, with Heracles, generous hospitality for the tramping hero becomes more than just a matter of correctness or etiquette when one thinks of such "hosts" as Procrustes, Sciron, and Antaeus. Violation of the rights of *xenia* is an underlying theme which directs the action in both the story of Troy and the story of Odysseus. The sin of Laomedon provoked divine rage against Troy; then Paris doomed the city when, after being properly received in the house of Menelaus, he went off with his host's wife and most of his furniture. Decisive for the action of the *Odyssey* is that travesty of *xenia* performed by the suitors when they settle down and make themselves intolerably at home in the house of Odysseus.

If we adopt the admittedly somewhat hypothetical scheme according to which tragedy consists in the destruction or self-destruction of an otherwise great man through some fault or flaw in his character, then *Alcestis* might be viewed as a kind of inverted tragedy. For this hero, otherwise no better than ordinary, has one significant *virtue*, which *saves* him. Thus, again, the progress of the play is from ruin to safety, reversing what might be considered the normal course of tragedy. I would not press this view, although I think there is a little truth in it, because Euripides would have had to have a formula for tragedy before he could invert it, and we do not know that he had such a formula. At any rate, the "comic" qualities of *Alcestis* have puzzled critics since ancient times. It was played fourth in the set, in the position usually given to a satyr-play. But attempts to explain *Alcestis* as a modified satyr-play are not convincing, and the comic elements are not highly significant. Heracles may momentarily be ? moderately funny drunk, but that is about all. The squabble between Admetus and Pheres, in which both really lose, is too humanly disagreeable to be funny; the squabble between Apollo and Death is grotesque, but scarcely uproarious. *Alcestis* is no satyr-play, but a tragi-comedy which in part (loss, escape, reunion) anticipates the lighter escape-dramas (*Iphigenia in Tauris, Helen*) still to come. But it goes deeper than these do.

Date and Circumstances

Alcestis was presented in 438 B.C. The first three plays in the set (all lost) were *The Women of Crete, Alcmaeon in Psophis,* and *Telephus.* Thus *Alcestis* is the earliest extant work of Euripides, with the possible exception of *The Cyclops* and (very doubtful) *Rhesus,* which are undated. Euripides won second place, being beaten by Sophocles.

Text

I have followed Murray's Oxford text, and used his line numbers, which are standard; except that I have adopted different readings which affect the translation of the following lines: 50, 124, 223, 943, 1140, 1153.

CHARACTERS

Apollo

Death

Chorus of citizens of Pherae

Maid, attendant of Alcestis

Alcestis, wife of Admetus

Admetus of Pherae, king of Thessaly

Boy (Eumelus), son of Admetus and Alcestis

Heracles

Pheres, father of Admetus

Servant of Admetus

*Girl, daughter of Admetus and Alcestis
    (silent character)*

Servants (silent)

ALCESTIS

SCENE: *Pherae, in Thessaly, before the house of Admetus. The front door of the house, or palace, is the center of the backdrop.*

(*Enter Apollo from the house, armed with a bow.*)

Apollo
House of Admetus, in which I, god though I am,
had patience to accept the table of the serfs!
Zeus was the cause. Zeus killed my son, Asclepius,
and drove the bolt of the hot lightning through his
   chest.
I, in my anger for this, killed the Cyclopes,   5
smiths of Zeus's fire, for which my father made me
   serve
a mortal man, in penance for my misdoings.
I came to this country, tended the oxen of this host
and friend, Admetus, son of Pheres. I have kept
his house from danger, cheated the Fates to save
   his life   10
until this day, for he revered my sacred rights
sacredly, and the fatal goddesses allowed
Admetus to escape the moment of his death
by giving the lower powers someone else to die
instead of him. He tried his loved ones all in turn,   15
father and aged mother who had given him birth,
and found not one, except his wife, who would
   consent
to die for him, and not see daylight any more.
She is in the house now, gathered in his arms and held
at the breaking point of life, because the destiny
   marks   20

this for her day of death and taking leave of life.
The stain of death in the house must not be on me. I
step therefore from these chambers dearest to my
  love.
And here is Death himself, I see him coming, Death
who dedicates the dying, who will lead her down   25
to the house of Hades. He has come on time. He has
been watching for this day on which her death
  falls due.

        (Enter Death, armed with a sword, from the
                wing. He sees Apollo suddenly and
                            shows surprise.)

Death
Ah!
You at this house, Phoebus? Why do you haunt
the place? It is unfair to take for your own   30
and spoil the death-spirits' privileges.
Was it not enough, then, that you blocked the death
of Admetus, and overthrew the Fates
by a shabby wrestler's trick? And now
your bow hand is armed to guard her too,   35
Alcestis, Pelias' daughter, though she
promised her life for her husband's.

Apollo
Never fear. I have nothing but justice and fair words
  for you.

Death
If you mean fairly, what are you doing with a bow?

Apollo
It is my custom to carry it with me all the time.   40

Death
It is your custom to help this house more than you
  ought.

Apollo
But he is my friend, and his misfortunes trouble me.

Death
You mean to take her body, too, away from me?

Apollo
I never took *his* body away from you by force.

Death
How is it, then, that he is above ground, not below?   45

Apollo
He gave his wife instead, and you have come for
  her now.

Death
I have. And I shall take her down where the dead are.

Apollo
Take her and go. I am not sure you will listen to me.

Death
Tell me to kill whom I must kill. Such are my orders.

Apollo
No, only to put their death off. They must die in
  the end.   50

Death
I understand what you would say and what you want.

Apollo
Is there any way, then, for Alcestis to grow old?

Death
There is not. I insist on enjoying my rights too.

Apollo
You would not take more than one life, in any case.

Death
My privilege means more to me when they die young.   55

Apollo
If she dies old, she will have a lavish burial.

Death
What you propose, Phoebus, is to favor the rich.

Apollo
What is this? Have you unrecognized talents for
debate?

Death
Those who could afford to buy a late death would buy
it then.

Apollo
I see. Are you determined not to do this for me?   60

Death
I will not do it. And you know my character.

Apollo
I know it: hateful to mankind, loathed by the gods.

Death
You cannot always have your way where you should
not.

Apollo
For all your brute ferocity you shall be stopped.
The man to do it is on the way to Pheres' house   65
now, on an errand from Eurystheus, sent to steal
a team of horses from the wintry lands of Thrace.
He shall be entertained here in Admetus' house
and he shall take the woman away from you by force,
nor will you have our gratitude, but you shall still   70
be forced to do it, and to have my hate beside.

Death
Much talk. Talking will win you nothing. All the
same,
the woman goes with me to Hades' house. I go
to take her now, and dedicate her with my sword,
for all whose hair is cut in consecration   75
by this blade's edge are devoted to the gods below.

(Death enters the house. Apollo leaves by the wing.
The Chorus enters and forms a group
before the gates.)

Chorus
It is quiet by the palace. What does it mean?
Why is the house of Admetus so still?
Is there none here of his family, none
who can tell us whether the queen is dead   80
and therefore to be mourned? Or does Pelias'
daughter Alcestis live still, still look
on daylight, she who in my mind appears
noble beyond
all women beside in a wife's duty?   85

(Here they speak individually, not as a group.)

First Citizen
Does someone hear anything?
The sound a hand's stroke would make,
or outcry, as if something were done
and over?

Second Citizen
        No. And there is no servant stationed
at the outer gates. O Paean,   90
healer, might you show in light
to still the storm of disaster.

Third Citizen
They would not be silent if she were dead.

Fourth Citizen
No, she is gone.

Fifth Citizen
They have not taken her yet from the house.

Sixth Citizen
So sure? I know nothing. Why are you certain?   95
And how could Admetus have buried his wife
with none by, and she so splendid?

Seventh Citizen
Here at the gates I do not see
the lustral spring water, approved
by custom for a house of death.   100

Eighth Citizen
Nor are there cut locks of hair at the forecourts
hanging, such as the stroke of sorrow
for the dead makes. I can hear no beating
of the hands of young women.

Ninth Citizen
Yet this is the day appointed.   105

Tenth Citizen
What do you mean? Speak.

Ninth Citizen
On which she must pass to the world below.

Eleventh Citizen
You touch me deep, my heart, where it hurts.

Twelfth Citizen
Yes. He who from the first has claimed to be called
a good man himself   110
must grieve when good men are afflicted.

(*Henceforward all the Chorus together*)

Sailing the long sea, there is
not any place on earth
you could win, not Lycia,
not the unwatered sands called   115
of Ammon, not
thus to approach and redeem the life
of this unhappy woman. Her fate shows
steep and near. There is no god's hearth
I know you could reach and by sacrifice   120
avail to save.

There was only one. If the eyes
of Phoebus' son were opened
still, if he could have come
and left the dark chambers,   125
the gates of Hades.
He upraised those who were stricken
down, until from the hand of God
the flown bolt of thunder hit him.
Where is there any hope for life   130
left for me any longer?

For all has been done that can be done by our kings
    now,
and there on all the gods' altars
are blood sacrifices dripping in full,
but no healing comes for the evil.   135

(*Enter a maid from the house.*)

Chorus
But here is a serving woman coming from the house.
The tears break from her. What will she say has
    taken place?
We must, of course, forgive your sorrow if something
has happened to your masters. We should like to know
whether the queen is dead or if she is still alive.   140

Maid
I could tell you that she is still alive or that she
    is dead.

Chorus
How could a person both be dead and live and see?

Maid
It has felled her, and the life is breaking from
    her now.

Chorus
Such a husband, to lose such a wife. I pity you.

13

Maid
The master does not see it and he will not see it   145
until it happens.

Chorus
> There is no hope left she will live?

Maid
None. This is the day of destiny. It is too strong.

Chorus
Surely, he must be doing all he can for her.

Maid
All is prepared so he can bury her in style.

Chorus
Let her be sure, at least, that as she dies, there dies   150
the noblest woman underneath the sun, by far.

Maid
Noblest? Of course the noblest, who will argue that?
What shall the wife be who surpasses her? And how
could any woman show that she loves her husband
    more
than herself better than by consent to die for him?   155
But all the city knows that well. You shall be told
now how she acted in the house, and be amazed
to hear. For when she understood the fatal day
was come, she bathed her white body with water
    drawn
from running streams, then opened the cedar chest
    and took   160
her clothes out, and dressed in all her finery
and stood before the Spirit in the Hearth, and prayed:
"Mistress, since I am going down beneath the ground,
I kneel before you in this last of all my prayers.
Take care of my children for me. Give the little girl   165
a husband; give the little boy a generous wife;
and do not let my children die like me, who gave
them birth, untimely. Let them live a happy life

14

through to the end and prosper here in their own
    land."

Afterward she approached the altars, all that stand   170
in the house of Admetus, made her prayers, and
    decked them all
with fresh sprays torn from living myrtle. And she
    wept
not at all, made no outcry. The advancing doom
made no change in the color and beauty of her face.
But then, in their room, she threw herself upon the
    bed,   175
and there she did cry, there she spoke: "O marriage
    bed,
it was here that I undressed my maidenhood and
    gave
myself up to this husband for whose sake I die.
Goodbye. I hold no grudge. But you have been my
    death
and mine alone. I could not bear to play him false.   180
I die. Some other woman will possess you now.
She will not be better, but she might be happier."
She fell on the bed and kissed it. All the coverings
were drenched in the unchecked outpouring of her
    tears;
but after much crying, when all her tears were shed,   185
she rolled from the couch and walked away with eyes
    cast down,
began to leave the room, but turned and turned again
to fling herself once more upon the bed. Meanwhile
the children clung upon their mother's dress, and
    cried,
until she gathered them into her arms, and kissed   190
first one and then the other, as in death's farewell.
And all the servants in the house were crying now
in sorrow for their mistress. Then she gave her hand
to each, and each one took it, there was none so mean
in station that she did not stop and talk with him.   195

This is what Admetus and the house are losing. Had
he died, he would have lost her, but in this escape
he will keep the pain. It will not ever go away.

Chorus
Admetus surely must be grieving over this
when such a wife must be taken away from him.   200

Maid
Oh yes, he is crying. He holds his wife close in
  his arms,
imploring her not to forsake him. What he wants
is impossible. She is dying. The sickness fades her
  now.
She has gone slack, just an inert weight on the arm.
Still, though so little breath of life is left in her,   205
she wants to look once more upon the light of the
  sun,
since this will be the last time of all, and never again.
She must see the sun's shining circle yet one more
  time.
Now I must go announce your presence. It is not
everyone who bears so much good will toward our
  kings   210
as to stand by ready to help in their distress.
But you have been my master's friends since long
  ago.

                                                    (*Exit.*)

Chorus
O Zeus, Zeus, what way out of this evil
is there, what escape from this
which is happening to our princess?
A way, any way? Must I cut short my hair   215
for grief, put upon me the black
costume that means mourning?
We must, friends, clearly we must; yet still
let us pray to the gods. The gods
have power beyond all power elsewhere.

Paean, my lord, 220
Apollo, make some way of escape for Admetus.
Grant it, oh grant it. Once you found
rescue in him. Be now
in turn his redeemer from death.
Oppose bloodthirsty Hades. 225

Admetus,
O son of Pheres, what a loss
to suffer, when such a wife goes.
A man could cut his throat for this, for this
and less he could bind the noose upon his neck
and hang himself. For this is 230
not only dear, but dearest of all,
this wife you will see dead
on this day before you.

> (*Alcestis is carried from the house on a litter,
> supported by Admetus and followed by her
> children and servants of the household.*)

But see, see,
she is coming out of the house and her husband is
 with her.
Cry out aloud, mourn, you land
of Pherae for the bravest 235
of wives fading in sickness and doomed
to the Death God of the world below.

I will never again say that marriage brings
more pleasure than pain. I judge by what
I have known in the past, an' by seeing now 240
what happens to our king, who is losing a wife
brave beyond all others, and must live a life
that will be no life for the rest of time.

Alcestis
Sun, and light of the day,
O turning wheel of the sky, clouds that fly. 245

Admetus

The sun sees you and me, two people suffering,
who never hurt the gods so they should make you die.

Alcestis

My land, and palace arching my land,
and marriage chambers of Iolcus, my own country.

Admetus

Raise yourself, my Alcestis, do not leave me now.   250
I implore the gods to pity you. They have the power.

Alcestis

I see him there at the oars of his little boat in
  the lake,
the ferryman of the dead,
Charon, with his hand upon the oar,
and he calls me now: "What keeps you?   255
Hurry, you hold us back." He is urging me on
in angry impatience.

Admetus

The crossing you speak of is a bitter one for me;
ill starred; it is unfair we should be treated so.

Alcestis

Somebody has me, somebody takes me away, do you
  see,
don't you see, to the courts   260
of dead men. He frowns from under dark
brows. He has wings. It is Death.
Let me go, what are you doing, let go.

                    Such is the road
most wretched I have to walk.

Admetus

Sorrow for all who love you, most of all for me
and for the children. All of us share in this grief.   265

Alcestis

Let me go now, let me down,

flat. I have no strength to stand.
Death is close to me.
The darkness creeps over my eyes. O children,
my children, you have no mother now,   270
not any longer. Daylight is yours,
my children. Look on it and be happy.

Admetus
Ah, a bitter word for me to hear,
heavier than any death of my own.
Before the gods, do not be so harsh   275
as to leave me, leave your children forlorn.
No, up, and fight it.
There would be nothing left of me if you died.
All rests in you, our life, our not
having life. Your love is our worship.

Alcestis
Admetus, you can see how it is with me. Therefore,   280
I wish to have some words with you before I die.
I put you first, and at the price of my own life
made certain you would live and see the daylight. So
I die, who did not have to die, because of you.
I could have taken any man in Thessaly   285
I wished and lived in queenly state here in this house.
But since I did not wish to live bereft of you
and with our children fatherless, I did not spare
my youth, although I had so much to live for. Yet
your father, and the mother who bore you, gave
   you up,   290
though they had reached an age when it was good
   to die
and good to save their son and end it honorably.
You were their only one, and they had no more hope
of having other children if you died. That way
I would be living and you would live the rest of
   our time,   295
and you would not be alone and mourning for your
   wife

and tending motherless children. No, but it must be
that some god has so wrought that things shall be
  this way.
So be it. But swear now to do, in recompense,
what I shall ask you—not enough, oh, never enough,   300
since nothing is enough to make up for a life,
but fair, and you yourself will say so, since you love
these children as much as I do; or at least you should.
Keep them as masters in my house, and do not marry
again and give our children to a stepmother   305
who will not be so kind as I, who will be jealous
and raise her hand to your children and mine. Oh no,
do not do that, do not. That is my charge to you.
For the new-come stepmother hates the children born
to a first wife, no viper could be deadlier.   310
The little boy has his father for a tower of strength.
[He can talk with him and be spoken to in turn.]
But you, my darling, what will your girlhood be like,
how will your father's new wife like you? She must
  not
make shameful stories up about you, and contrive   315
to spoil your chance of marriage in the blush of youth,
because your mother will not be there to help you
when you are married, not be there to give you
  strength
when your babies are born, when only a mother's
  help will do.
For I must die. It will not be tomorrow, not   320
the next day, or this month, the horrible thing will
  come,
but now, at once, I shall be counted among the dead.
Goodbye, be happy, both of you. And you, my husband,
can boast the bride you took made you the bravest
  wife,
and you, children, can say, too, that your mother
  was brave.   325

Chorus
Fear nothing; for I dare to speak for him. He will
do all you ask. If he does not the fault is his.

Admetus
It shall be so, it shall be, do not fear, since you
were mine in life, you still shall be my bride in death
and you alone, no other girl in Thessaly   330
shall ever be called wife of Admetus in your place.
There is none such, none so marked out in pride of
    birth
nor beauty's brilliance, nor in anything else. I have
these children, they are enough; I only pray the gods
grant me the bliss to keep them as we could not
    keep you.   335
I shall go into mourning for you, not for just
a year, but all my life while it still lasts, my dear,
and hate the woman who gave me birth always, detest
my father. These were called my own people. They
    were not.

You gave what was your own and dear to buy my life   340
and saved me. Am I not to lead a mourning life
when I have lost a wife like you? I shall make an end
of revelry and entertainment in my house,
the flowers and the music that were found here once.
No, I shall never touch the lutestrings ever again   345
nor have the heart to play music upon the flute
of Libya, for you took my joy in life with you.
I shall have the skilled hand of an artificer
make me an image of you to set in my room,
pay my devotions to it, hold it in my arms   350
and speak your name, and clasp it close against my
    heart,
and think I hold my wife again, though I do not,
cold consolation, I know it, and yet even so
I might drain the weight of sorrow. You could come
to see me in my dreams and comfort me. For they   355

21

who love find a time's sweetness in the visions of
    night.
Had I the lips of Orpheus and his melody
to charm the maiden daughter of Demeter and
her lord, and by my singing win you back from death,
I would have gone beneath the earth, and not the
    hound   360
of Pluto could have stayed me, not the ferryman
of ghosts, Charon at his oar. I would have brought
    you back
to life. Wait for me, then, in that place, till I die,
and make ready the room where you will live
    with me,
for I shall have them bury me in the same chest   365
as you, and lay me at your side, so that my heart
shall be against your heart, and never, even in death,
shall I go from you. You alone were true to me.

Chorus
And I, because I am your friend and you
are mine, shall help you bear this sorrow, as I should.   370

Alcestis
Children, you now have heard your father promise me
that he will never marry again and not inflict
a new wife on you, but will keep my memory.

Admetus
I promise. I will keep my promise to the end.

Alcestis
On this condition, take the children. They are yours.   375

Admetus
I take them, a dear gift from a dear hand.

Alcestis
                           And now
you must be our children's mother, too, instead of me.

Admetus

I must be such, since they will no longer have you.

Alcestis

O children, this was my time to live, and I must go.

Admetus

Ah me, what shall I do without you all alone?   380

Alcestis

Time will soften it. The dead count for nothing at all.

Admetus

Oh, take me with you, for God's love, take me
   there too.

Alcestis

No, I am dying in your place. That is enough.

Admetus

O God, what a wife you are taking away from me.

Alcestis

It is true. My eyes darken and the heaviness comes.   385

Admetus

But I am lost, dear, if you leave me.

Alcestis

                                      There is no use
in talking to me any more. I am not there.

Admetus

No, lift your head up, do not leave your children thus.

Alcestis

I do not want to, but it is goodbye, children.

Admetus

Look at them, oh look at them.

Alcestis

                              No. There is nothing more.   390

Admetus
Are you really leaving us?

Alcestis

Goodbye.

Admetus

Oh, I am lost.

Chorus
It is over now. Admetus' wife is gone from us.

Boy
O wicked fortune. Mother has gone down there,
father, she is not here with us
in the sunshine any more.   395
She was cruel and went away
and left me to live all alone.
Look at her eyes, look at her hands, so still.
Hear me, mother, listen to me, oh please,   400
listen, it is I, mother,
I your little one lean and kiss
your lips, and cry out to you.

Admetus
She does not see, she does not hear you. You and I
both have a hard and heavy load to carry now.   405

Boy
Father, I am too small to be left alone
by the mother I loved so much. Oh,
it is hard for me to bear
all this that is happening,
and you, little sister, suffer   410
with me too. Oh, father,
your marriage was empty, empty, she did not live
to grow old with you.
She died too soon. Mother, with you gone away,
the whole house is ruined.   415

24

(Alcestis is carried into the house, followed
by children and servants.)

Chorus

Admetus, you must stand up to misfortune now.
You are not the first, and not the last of humankind
to lose a good wife. Therefore, you must understand
death is an obligation claimed from all of us.

Admetus

I understand it. And this evil which has struck 420
was no surprise. I knew about it long ago,
and knowledge was hard. But now, since we must
  bury our dead,
stay with me and stand by me, chant responsively
the hymn of the unsacrificed-to-god below.
To all Thessalians over whom my rule extends 425
I ordain a public mourning for my wife, to be
observed with shaving of the head and with black
  robes.
The horses that you drive in chariots and those
you ride single shall have their manes cut short with
  steel,
and there shall be no sound of flutes within the city, 430
no sound of lyres, until twelve moons have filled and
  gone;
for I shall never bury any dearer dead
than she, nor any who loved me better. She deserves
my thanks. She died for me, which no one else
  would do.

(Exit into the house.)

Chorus

O daughter of Pelias 435
my wish for you is a happy life
in the sunless chambers of Hades.
Now let the dark-haired lord of Death himself, and
  the old man,

25

who sits at the steering oar   440
and ferries the corpses,
know that you are the bravest of wives, by far,
ever conveyed across the tarn
of Acheron in the rowboat.

Much shall be sung of you   445
by the men of music to the seven-strung mountain
lyre-shell, and in poems that have no music,
in Sparta when the season turns and the month
    Carneian
comes back, and the moon
rides all the night;   450
in Athens also, the shining and rich.
Such is the theme of song you left
in death, for the poets.

Oh that it were in my power   455
and that I had strength to bring you
back to light from the dark of death
with oars on the sunken river.
For you, O dearest among women, you only   460
had the hard courage
to give your life for your husband's and save
him from death. May the dust lie light
upon you, my lady. And should he now take
a new wife to his bed, he will win my horror and
    hatred,
mine, and your children's hatred too.   465

His mother would not endure
to have her body hidden in the ground
for him, nor the aged father
He was theirs, but they had not courage to save him.
Oh shame, for the gray was upon them.   470
But you, in the pride
of youth, died for him and left the daylight.
May it only be mine to win
such wedded love as hers from a wife; for this

is given seldom to mortals; but were my wife such,
   I would have her
with me unhurt through her lifetime.   475

(*Enter Heracles from the road, travel-stained.*)

Heracles
My friends, people of Phera- and the villages
hereby, tell me, shall I find Admetus at home?

Chorus
Yes, Heracles, the son of Pheres is in the house.
But tell us, what is the errand that brings you here
to Thessaly and the city of Pherae once again?   480

Heracles
I have a piece of work to do for Eurystheus
of Tiryns.

Chorus
        Where does it take you? On what far journey?

Heracles
To Thrace, to take home Diomedes' chariot.

Chorus
How can you? Do you know the man you are to meet?

Heracles
No. I have never been where the Bistones live.   485

Chorus
You cannot master his horses. Not without a fight.

Heracles
It is my work, and I cannot refuse.

Chorus
                                You must
kill him before you come back; or be killed and stay.

Heracles
If I must fight, it will not be for the first time.

Chorus
What good will it do you if you overpower their
    master?   490

Heracles
I will take the horses home to Tiryns and its king.

Chorus
It is not easy to put a bridle on their jaws.

Heracles
Easy enough, unless their nostrils are snorting fire.

Chorus
Not that, but they have teeth that tear a man apart.

Heracles
Oh no! Mountain beasts, not horses, feed like that.   495

Chorus
But you can see their mangers. They are caked with
    blood.

Heracles
And the man who raises them? Whose son does he
    claim he is?

Chorus
Ares'. And he is lord of the golden shield of Thrace.

Heracles
It sounds like my life and the kind of work I do.
It is a hard and steep way always that I go,   500
having to fight one after another all the sons
the war god ever got him, with Lycaon first,
again with Cycnus, and now here is a third fight
that I must have with the master of these horses. So—
I am Alcmene's son, and the man does not live   505
who will see me break before my enemy's attack.

Chorus
Here is the monarch of our country coming
from the house himself, Admetus.

28

(Enter Admetus.)

Admetus

                    Welcome and happiness
to you, O scion of Perseus' blood and child of Zeus.

Heracles

Happiness to you likewise, lord of Thessaly,   510
Admetus.

Admetus

        I could wish it. I know you mean well.

Heracles

What is the matter? Why is there mourning and
  cut hair?

Admetus

There is one dead here whom I must bury today.

Heracles

Not one of your children! I pray God shield them
  from that.

Admetus

Not they. My children are well and living in their
  house.   515

Heracles

If it is your father who is gone, his time was ripe.

Admetus

No, he is still there, Heracles. My mother, too.

Heracles

Surely you have not lost your wife, Alcestis.

Admetus

                            Yes
and no. There are two ways that I could answer that.

Heracles

Did you say that she is dead or that she is still alive?   520

29

Admetus
She is, but she is gone away. It troubles me.

Heracles
I still do not know what you mean. You are being
obscure.

Admetus
You know about her and what must happen, do
you not?

Heracles
I know that she has undertaken to die for you.

Admetus
How can she really live, then, when she has promised
that?   525

Heracles
Ah, do not mourn her before she dies. Wait for the
time.

Admetus
The point of death is death, and the dead are lost
and gone.

Heracles
Being and nonbeing are considered different things.

Admetus
That is your opinion, Heracles. It is not mine.

Heracles
Well, but whose is the mourning now? Is it in the
family?   530

Admetus
A woman. We were speaking of a woman, were we
not?

Heracles
Was she a blood relative or someone from outside?

Admetus
No relation by blood, but she meant much to us.

Heracles
How does it happen that she died here in your house?

Admetus
She lost her father and came here to live with us.   535

Heracles
I am sorry,
Admetus. I wish I had found you in a happier state.

Admetus
Why do you say that? What do you mean to do?

Heracles
                                        I mean
to go on, and stay with another of my friends.

Admetus
No, my lord, no. The evil must not come to that.

Heracles
The friend who stays with friends in mourning is in
   the way.   540

Admetus
The dead are dead. Go on in.

Heracles
                         No. It is always wrong
for guests to revel in a house where others mourn.

Admetus
There are separate guest chambers. We can take you
   there.

Heracles
Let me go, and I will thank you a thousand times.

Admetus
You shall not go to stay with any other man.   545

You there: open the guest rooms which are across
   the court
from the house, and tell the people who are there to
   provide
plenty to eat, and make sure that you close the doors
facing the inside court. It is not right for guests
to have their pleasures interrupted by sounds of grief.   550

(*Heracles is ushered inside.*)

Chorus
Admetus, are you crazy? What are you thinking of
to entertain guests in a situation like this?

Admetus
And if I had driven from my city and my house
the guest and friend who came to me, would you have
   approved
of me more? Wrong. My misery would still have been   555
as great, and I should be inhospitable too,
and there would be one more misfortune added to
   those
I have, if my house is called unfriendly to its friends.
For this man is my best friend, and he is my host
whenever I go to Argos, which is a thirsty place.   560

Chorus
Yes, but then why did you hide what is happening
   here
if this visitor is, as you say, your best friend?

Admetus
He would not have been willing to come inside my
   house
if he had known what trouble I was in. I know.
There are some will think I show no sense in doing
   this.   565
They will not like it. But my house does not know
   how

to push its friends away and not treat them as it
should.

(*He goes inside.*)

Chorus
O liberal and forever free-handed house of this man,
the Pythian himself, lyric Apollo,   570
was pleased to live with you
and had patience upon you. lands
to work as a shepherd,
and on the hill-folds and the slopes   575
piped to the pasturing of your flocks
in their season of mating.
And even dappled lynxes for delight in his melody
joined him as shepherds. From the cleft of Othrys
   descended   580
a red troop of lions,
and there, Phoebus, to your lyre's strain
there danced the bright-coated
fawn, adventuring from the deep   585
bearded pines, lightfooted for joy
in your song, in its kindness.

Therefore, your house is beyond
all others for wealth of flocks by the sweet waters
of Lake Boebias. For spread of cornland   590
and pasturing range its boundary stands
only there where the sun
stalls his horses in dark air by the Molossians.
Eastward he sways all to the harborless   595
Pelian coast on the Aegaean main.

Now he has spread wide his doors
and taken the guest in, when his eyes were wet
and he wept still for a beloved wife who died
in the house so lately. The noble strain   600
comes out, in respect for others.
All that wisdom means is there in the noble. I stand

in awe, and good hope has come again to my heart
that for this godly man the end will be good.   605

*(Enter Admetus from the house, followed by
servants with a covered litter.)*

Admetus
Gentlemen of Pherae, I am grateful for your company.
My men are bearing to the burning place and grave
our dead, who now has all the state which is her due.
Will you then, as the custom is among us, say
farewell to the dead as she goes forth for the last
    time?   610

Chorus
Yes, but I see your father coming now. He walks
as old men do, and followers carry in their hands
gifts for your wife, to adorn her in the underworld.

(Enter Pheres, attended, from outside.)

Pheres
I have come to bear your sorrows with you, son.
    I know,
nobody will dispute it, you have lost a wife   615
both good and modest in her ways. Nevertheless,
you have to bear it, even though it is hard to bear.
Accept these gifts to deck her body, bury them
with her. Oh yes, she well deserves honor in death.
She died to save your life, my son. She would not let   620
me be a childless old man, would not let me waste
away in sorrowful age deprived of you. Thereby,
daring this generous action, she has made the life
of all women become a thing of better repute
than it was.

　　　　O you who saved him, you who raised us up   625
when we were fallen, farewell, even in Hades' house
may good befall you.

　　　　　　I say people ought to marry women
like this. Otherwise, better not to marry at all.

Admetus

I never invited you to come and see her buried,
nor do I count your company as that of a friend.   630
She shall not wear anything that you bring her.
She needs nothing from you to be buried in. Your
    time
to share my sorrow was when I was about to die.
But you stood out of the way and let youth take my
    place
in death, though you were old. Will you cry for her
    now?   635
It cannot be that my body ever came from you,
nor did the woman who claims she bore me and
    is called
my mother give me birth. I was got from some slave
and surreptitiously put to your wife to nurse.
You show it. Your nature in the crisis has come out.   640
I do not count myself as any child of yours.
Oh, you outpass the cowardice of all the world,
you at your age, come to the very last step of life
and would not, dared not, die for your own child.
    Oh, no,
you let this woman, married into our family,   645
do it instead, and therefore it is right for me
to call her all the father and mother that I have.
And yet you two should honorably have striven for
the right of dying for your child. The time of life
you had left for your living was short, in any case,   650
and she and I would still be living out our time
and I should not be hurt and grieving over her.
And yet, all that a man could have to bless his life
you have had. You had your youth in kingship. There
    was I
your son, ready to take it over, keep your house   655
in order, so you had no childless death to fear,
with the house left to be torn apart by other claims.
You cannot justify your leaving me to death
on grounds that I disrespected your old age. Always I

35

showed all consideration. See what thanks I get   660
from you and from the woman who gave me birth.
  Go on,
get you other children, you cannot do it too soon,
who will look after your old age, and lay you out
when you are dead, and see you buried properly.
I will not do it. This hand will never bury you.   665
I am dead as far as you are concerned, and if, because
I found another savior, I still look on the sun,
I count myself that person's child and fond support.
It is meaningless, the way th. old men pray for death
and complain of age and the long time they have
  to live.   670
Let death only come close, not one of them still wants
to die. Their age is not a burden any more.

Chorus

Stop, stop. We have trouble enough already, child.
You will exasperate your father with this talk.

Pheres

Big words, son. Who do you think you are cursing out   675
like this? Some Lydian slave, some Phrygian that
  you bought?
I am a free Thessalian noble, nobly born
from a Thessalian. Are you forgetting that? You go
too far with your high-handedness. You volley brash
words at me, and fail to hit me, and then run away.   680
I gave you life, and made you master of my house,
and raised you. I am not obliged to die for you.
I do not acknowledge any tradition among us
that fathers should die for their sons. That is not
  Greek.
Your natural right is to find your own happiness   685
or unhappiness. All you deserve from me, you have.
You are lord of many. I have wide estates of land
to leave you, just as my father left them to me.
What harm have I done you then? What am I taking
  away

36

from you? Do not die for me I will not die for you.   690
You like the sunlight. Don't you think your father
   does?
I count the time I have to spend down there as long,
and the time to live is little, but that little is sweet.
You fought shamelessly for a way to escape death,
and passed your proper moment, and are still alive   695
because you killed her. Then, you wretch, you dare
   to call
me coward, when you let your woman outdare you,
and die for her magnificent young man? I see.
You have found a clever scheme by which you *never*
   will die.
You will always persuade the wife you have at the
   time   700
to die for you instead. And you, so low, then dare
blame your own people for not wanting to do this.
Silence. I tell you, as you cherish your own life,
all other people cherish theirs. And if you call
us names, you will be called names, and the names
   are true.   705

Chorus
Too much evil has been said in this speech and in
that spoken before. Old sir, stop cursing your own
   son.

Admetus
No, speak, and I will speak too. If it hurts to hear
the truth, you should not have made a mistake
   with me.

Pheres
I should have made a mistake if I had died for you.   710

Admetus
Is it the same thing to die old and to die young?

Pheres
Yes. We have only one life and not two to live.

Admetus
I think you would like to live a longer time than Zeus.

Pheres
Cursing your parents, when they have done nothing
to you?

Admetus
Yes, for I found you much in love with a long life.   715

Pheres
Who is it you are burying? Did not someone die?

Admetus
And that she died, you foul wretch, proves your
cowardice.

Pheres
You cannot say that we were involved in her death.

Admetus
Ah.
I hope that some day you will stand in need of me.   720

Pheres
Go on, and court more women, so they all can die.

Admetus
Your fault. You were not willing to.

Pheres
                              No, I was not.
It is a sweet thing, this God's sunshine, sweet to see.

Admetus
That is an abject spirit, not a man's.

Pheres
                              You shall
not mock an old man while you carry out your dead.

Admetus
You will die in evil memory, when you do die.   725

Pheres
I do not care what they say of me when I am dead.

Admetus
How old age loses all the sense of shame.

Pheres

                              She was
not shameless, you found; she was only innocent.

Admetus
Get out of here now and let me bury my dead.

Pheres
I'll go. You murdered her, and you can bury her.   730
But you will have her brothers still to face. You'll pay,
for Acastus is no longer counted as a man
unless he sees you punished for his sister's blood.

Admetus
Go and be damned, you and that woman who lives
   with you.
Grow old as you deserve, childless, although your son   735
still lives. You shall not come again under the same
   roof
with me. And if I had to proclaim by heralds that I
disowned my father's house, I should have so pro-
   claimed.

                    (*Pheres goes off.*)

Now we, for we must bear the sorrow that is ours,
shall go, and lay her body on the burning place.   740

Chorus
Ah, cruel the price of your daring,
O generous one, O noble and brave,
farewell. May Hermes of the world below
and Hades welcome you. And if, even there,
the good fare best, may you have high honor   745
and sit by the bride of Hades.

(The body is borne off, followed by Admetus, servants, and Chorus. Thus the stage is empty. Then enter, from the house, the servant who was put in charge of Heracles.)

Servant

I have known all sorts of foreigners who have come in
from all over the world here to Admetus' house,
and I have served them dinner, but I never yet
have had a guest as bad as this to entertain.   750
In the first place, he could see the master was in
   mourning,
but inconsiderately came in anyway.
Then, he refused to understand the situation
and be content with anything we could provide,
but when we failed to bring him something, de-
   manded it,   755
and took a cup with ivy on it in both hands
and drank the wine of our dark mother, straight, until
the flame of the wine went all through him, and
   heated him,
and then he wreathed branches of myrtle on his head
and howled, off key. There were two kinds of music
   now   760
to hear, for while he sang and never gave a thought
to the sorrows of Admetus, we servants were mourning
our mistress; but we could not show before our guest
with our eyes wet. Admetus had forbidden that.
So now I have to entertain this guest inside,   765
this ruffian thief, this highwayman, whatever he is,
while she is gone away from the house, and I
   could not
say goodbye, stretch my hand out to her in my grief
for a mistress who was like a mother to all the house
and me. She gentled her husband's rages, saved us all   770
from trouble after trouble. Am I not then right
to hate this guest who has come here in our miseries?

(Enter Heracles from the house, drunk,
but not hopelessly so.)

Heracles

You there, with the sad and melancholy face, what is
the matter with you? The servant who looks after
  guests
should be polite and cheerful and not scowl at them.   775
But look at you. Here comes your master's dearest
  friend
to visit you, and you receive him with black looks
and frowns, all because of some trouble somewhere
  else.
Come here, I'll tell you something that will make
  you wise.
Do you really know what things are like, the way
  they are?   780
I don't think so. How could you? Well, then, listen
  to me.
Death is an obligation which we all must pay.
There is not one man living who can truly say
if he will be alive or dead on the next day.
Fortune is dark; she moves, but we cannot see the way   785
nor can we pin her down by science and study her.
There, I have told you. Now you can understand.
  Go on,
enjoy yourself, drink, call the life you live today
your own, but only that, the rest belongs to chance.
Then, beyond all gods, pay your best attentions to   790
the Cyprian, man's sweetest. There's a god who's kind.
Let all this business go and do as I prescribe
for you, that is, if I seem to talk sense. Do I?
I think so. Well, then, get rid of this too-much grief,
put flowers on your head and drink with us, fight
  down   795
these present troubles; later, I know very well
that the wine splashing in the bowl will shake you
  loose

41

from these scowl-faced looks and the tension in your
   mind.
We are only human. Our thoughts should be human
   too,
since, for these solemn people and these people who
   scowl,   800
the whole parcel of them, if I am any judge,
life is not really life but a catastrophe.

Servant
I know all that. But we have troubles on our hands
now, that make revelry and laughter out of place.

Heracles
The dead woman is out of the family. Do not mourn   805
too hard. The master and the mistress are still alive.

Servant
What do you mean, alive? Do you not know what
   happened?

Heracles
Certainly, unless your master has lied to me.

Servant
He is too hospitable, too much.

Heracles
                      Should I not then
have enjoyed myself, because some outside woman
   was dead?   810

Servant
She was an outsider indeed. That is too true.

Heracles
Has something happened that he did not tell me
   about?

Servant
Never mind. Go. Our masters' sorrows are our own.

Heracles
These can be no outsiders' troubles.

Servant

                                        If they were,
I should not have minded seeing you enjoy yourself.   815

Heracles
Have I been scandalously misled by my own friends?

Servant
You came here when we were not prepared to take
   in guests.
You see, we are in mourning. You can see our robes
of black, and how our hair is cut short.

Heracles

                                   Who is dead?
The aged father? One of the children who is gone?   820

Servant
My lord, Admetus' wife is dead.

Heracles

                              What are you saying?
And all this time you were making me comfortable?

Servant
He could not bear to turn you from this house of his.

Heracles
My poor Admetus, what a helpmeet you have lost!

Servant
We are all dead and done for, not only she.   825

Heracles
I really knew it when I saw the tears in his eyes,
his shorn hair and his face; but he persuaded me
with talk of burying someone who was not by blood
related. So, unwillingly, I came inside
and drank here in the house of this hospitable man   830

when he was in this trouble! Worse, I wreathed my
head
with garlands, and drank freely. But you might have
said
something about this great disaster in the house.
Now, where shall I find her? Where is the funeral
being held?

Servant

Go straight along the Larisa road, and when you clear   835
the city you will see the monument and the mound.

> (*He goes into the house, leaving Heracles
> alone on the stage.*)

Heracles

O heart of mine and hand of mine, who have endured
so much already, prove what kind of son it was
Alcmene, daughter of Electryon, bore to Zeus
in Tiryns. I must save this woman who has died   840
so lately, bring Alcestis back to live in this house,
and pay Admetus all the kindness that I owe.
I must go there and watch for Death of the black
robes,
master of dead men, and I think I shall find him
drinking the blood of slaughtered beasts beside the
grave.   845
Then, if I can break suddenly from my hiding place,
catch him, and hold him in the circle of these arms,
there is no way he will be able to break my hold
on his bruised ribs, until he gives the woman up
to me. But if I miss my quarry, if he does not come   850
to the clotted offering, I must go down, I must ask
the Maiden and the Master in the sunless homes
of those below; and I have confidence I shall bring
Alcestis back, and give her to the arms of my friend
who did not drive me off but took me into his house   855
and, though he staggered under the stroke of circum-
stance,

hid it, for he was noble and respected me.
Who in all Thessaly is a truer friend than this?
Who in all Greece? Therefore, he must not ever say
that, being noble, he befriended a worthless man.   860

(*He goes out. Presently Admetus comes on,
followed by the Chorus.*)

Admetus
Hateful is this
return, hateful the sight of this house
widowed, empty. Where shall I go?
Where shall I stay? What shall I say?
How can I die?
My mother bore me to a heavy fate.   865
I envy the dead. I long for those
who are gone, to live in their houses, with them.
There is no pleasure in the sunshine
nor the feel of the hard earth under my feet.
Such was the hostage Death has taken   870
from me, and given to Hades.

(*As they chant this, Admetus moans inarticulately.*)

Chorus
Go on, go on. Plunge in the deep of the house.
What you have suffered is enough for tears.
You have gone through pain, I know,
but you do no good to the woman who lies   875
below. Never again to look on the face
of the wife you loved hurts you.

Admetus
You have opened the wound torn in my heart.
What can be worse for a man than to lose
a faithful wife? I envy those   880
without wives, without children. I wish I had not
ever married her, lived with her in this house.
We have each one life. To grieve for this
is burden enough.

45

When we could live single all our days   885
without children, it is not to be endured
to see children sicken or married love
despoiled by death.

                              (*As before.*)

Chorus
Chance comes. It is hard to wrestle against it.
There is no limit to set on your pain.   890
The weight is heavy. Yet still
bear up. You are not the first man to lose
his wife. Disaster appears, to crush
one man now, but afterward another.

Admetus
How long my sorrows, the pain for my loves   895
down under the earth.
Why did you stop me from throwing myself
in the hollow cut of the grave, there to lie
dead beside her, who was best on earth?
Then Hades would have held fast two lives,   900
not one, and the truest of all, who crossed
the lake of the dead together.

Chorus
There was a man
of my people, who lost a boy
any house would mourn for,   905
the only child. But still
he carried it well enough, though childless,
and he stricken with age
and the hair gray on him,
well on through his lifetime.   910

Admetus
O builded house, how shall I enter you?
How live, with this turn
of my fortune? How different now and then.
Then it was with Pelian pine torches,   915

46

with marriage songs, that I entered my house,
with the hand of a sweet bride on my arm,
with loud rout of revelers following
to bless her who now is dead, and me,
for our high birth, for nobilities   920
from either side which were joined in us.
Now the bridal chorus has changed for a dirge,
and for white robes the costumed black
goes with me inside
to where her room stands deserted.   925

Chorus
Your luck had been
good, so you were inexperienced when
grief came. Still you saved
your own life and substance.
Your wife is dead, your love forsaken.   930
What is new in this? Before
now death has parted
many from their wives.

Admetus
Friends, I believe my wife is happier than I   935
although I know she does not seem to be. For her,
there will be no more pain to touch her ever again.
She has her glory and is free from much distress.
But I, who should not be alive, who have passed by
my moment, shall lead a sorry life. I see it now.   940
How can I bear to go inside this house again?
Whom shall I speak to, who will speak to me, to give
me any pleasure in coming home? Where shall
  I turn?
The desolation in my house will drive me out
when I see my wife's bed empty, when I see the chairs   945
she used to sit in, and all about the house the floor
unwashed and dirty, while the children at my knees
huddle and cry for their mother and the servants
  mourn
their mistress and remember what the house has lost.

47

So it will be at home, but if I go outside   950
meeting my married friends in Thessaly, the sight
of their wives will drive me back, for I cannot endure
to look at my wife's agemates and the friends of her
  youth.
And anyone who hates me will say this of me:
"Look at the man, disgracefully alive, who dared   955
not die, but like a coward gave his wife instead
and so escaped death. Do you call him a man at all?
He turns on his own parents, but he would not die
himself." Besides my other troubles, they will speak
about me thus. What have I gained by living,
  friends,   960
when reputation, life, and action all are bad?

Chorus
I myself, in the transports
of mystic verses, as in study
of history and science, have found
nothing so strong as Compulsion,   965
nor any means to combat her,
not in the Thracian books set down
in verse by the school of Orpheus,
not in all the remedies Phoebus has given the heirs   970
of Asclepius to fight the many afflictions of man.

She alone is a goddess
without altar or image to pray
before. She heeds no sacrifice.   975
Majesty, bear no harder
on me than you have in my life before!
All Zeus even ordains
only with you is accomplished.
By strength you fold and crumple the steel of the
  Chalybes.   980
There is no pity in the sheer barrier of your will.

> (*They turn and speak directly to Admetus, who
> remains in the background.*)

Now she has caught your wife in the breakless grip
  of her hands.
Take it. You will never bring back, by crying,   985
the dead into the light again.
Even the sons of the gods fade
and go in death's shadow.   990
She was loved when she was with us.
She shall be loved still, now she is dead.
It was the best of all women to whom you were
  joined in marriage.

The monument of your wife must not be counted
  among the graves   995
of the dead, but it must be given its honors
as gods are, worship of wayfarers.
And as they turn the bend of the road   1000
and see it, men shall say:
"She died for the sake of her husband.
Now she is a blessed spirit.
Hail, majesty, be gracious to us." Thus will men
  speak in her presence.   1005

But here is someone who looks like Alcmene's son,
Admetus. He seems on his way to visit you.

> (*Heracles enters, leading a veiled woman
> by the hand.*)

Heracles
A man, Admetus, should be allowed to speak his mind
to a friend, instead of keeping his complaints sup-
  pressed
inside him. Now, I thought I had the right to stand   1010
beside you and endure what you endured, so prove
my friendship. But you never told me that she,
  who lay
dead, was your wife, but entertained me in your
  house
as if your mourning were for some outsider's death.

And so I wreathed my head and poured libations out   1015
to the gods, in your house, though your house had
    suffered so.
This was wrong, wrong I tell you, to have treated me
thus, though I have no wish to hurt you in your grief.
Now, as for the matter of why I have come back
    again,
I will tell you. Take this woman, keep her safe for me,   1020
until I have killed the master of the Bistones
and come back, bringing with me the horses of
    Thrace.
If I have bad luck—I hope not, I hope to come
back home—I give her to the service of your house.
It cost a struggle for her to come into my hands.   1025
You see, I came on people who were holding games
for all comers, with prizes which an athlete might
well spend an effort winning.

(*Points to the woman.*)

                        Here is the prize I won
and bring you. For the winners in the minor events
were given horses to take away, while those who won   1030
the heavier stuff, boxing and wrestling, got oxen,
and a woman was thrown in with them. Since I
    happened
to be there, it seemed wrong to let this splendid prize
go by. As I said, the woman is for you to keep.
She is not stolen. It cost me hard work to bring   1035
her here. Some day, perhaps, you will say I have
    done well.

Admetus

I did not mean to dishonor nor belittle you
when I concealed the fate of my unhappy wife,
but it would have added pain to pain already there
if you had been driven to shelter with some other host.   1040
This sorrow is mine. It is enough for me to weep.
As for the woman, if it can be done, my lord,

I beg you, have some other Thessalian, who has not
suffered as I have, keep her. You have many friends
in Pherae. Do not bring my sorrows back to me.   1045
I would not have strength to see her in my house
    and keep
my eyes dry. I am weak now. Do not add weakness
to my weakness. I have sorrow enough to weigh me
    down.
And where could a young woman live in this house?
    For
she is young, I can see it in her dress, her style.   1050
Am I to put her in the same quarters with the men?
And how, circulating among young men, shall she
    be kept
from harm? Not easy, Heracles, to hold in check
a young strong man. I am thinking of your interests.
Or shall I put her in my lost wife's chamber, keep   1055
her there? How can I take her to Alcestis' bed?
I fear blame from two quarters, from my countrymen
who might accuse me of betraying her who helped
me most, by running to the bed of another girl,
and from the dead herself. Her honor has its claim   1060
on me. I must be very careful. You, lady,
whoever you are, I tell you that you have the form
of my Alcestis; all your body is like hers.
Too much. Oh, for God's pity, take this woman away
out of my sight. I am beaten already, do not beat   1065
me again. For as I look on her, I think I see
my wife. It churns my heart to tumult, and the tears
break streaming from my eyes. How much must
    I endure
the bitter taste of sorrow which is still so fresh?

Chorus

I cannot put a good name to your fortune; yet   1070
whoever you are, you must endure what the god gives.

Heracles

I only wish that my strength had been great enough

for me to bring your wife back from the chambered
 deep
into the light. I would have done that grace for you.

Admetus
I know you would have wanted to. Why speak of it?   1075
There is no way for the dead to come back to the
 light.

Heracles
Then do not push your sorrow. Bear it as you must.

Admetus
Easier to comfort than to suffer and be strong.

Heracles
But if you wish to mourn for always, what will you
 gain?

Admetus
Nothing. I know it. But some impulse of my love   1080
makes me.

Heracles
    Why, surely. Love for the dead is cause for tears.

Admetus
Her death destroyed me, even more than I can say.

Heracles
You have lost a fine wife. Who will say you have not?

Admetus
                                    So fine
that I, whom you see, never shall be happy again.

Heracles
Time will soften it. The evil still is young and strong.   1085

Admetus
You can say time will soften it, if time means death.

Heracles
A wife, love, your new marriage will put an end
  to this.

Admetus
Silence! I never thought you would say a thing like
  that.

Heracles
What? You will not remarry but keep an empty bed?

Admetus
No woman ever shall sleep in my arms again.   1090

Heracles
Do you believe you help the dead by doing this?

Admetus
Wherever she may be, she deserves my honors still.

Heracles
Praiseworthy, yes, praiseworthy. And yet foolish, too.

Admetus
Call me so, then, but never call me bridegroom.

Heracles
I admire you for your faith and love you bear your
  wife.   1095

Admetus
Let me die if I betray her, though she is gone.

Heracles
                              Well then,
receive this woman into your most generous house.

Admetus
Please, in the name of Zeus your father, no!

Heracles
                              And yet
you will be making a mistake if you do not;

Admetus
and eaten at the heart with anguish if I do.   1100

Heracles
Obey. The grace of this may come where you need
   grace.

Admetus
Ah.
I wish you had never won her in those games of
   yours.

Heracles
Where I am winner, you are winner along with me.

Admetus
Honorably said. But let the woman go away.

Heracles
She will go, if she should. First look. See if she
   should.   1105

Admetus
She should, unless it means you will be angry
   with me.

Heracles
Something I know of makes me so insistent with you.

Admetus
So, have your way. But what you do does not
   please me.

Heracles
The time will come when you will thank me. Only
   obey.

Admetus (*to attendants*)
Escort her in, if she must be taken into this house.   1110

Heracles
I will not hand this lady over to attendants.

Admetus
You yourself lead her into the house then, if you
  wish.

Heracles
I will put her into your hands and into yours alone.

Admetus
I will not touch her. But she is free to come inside.

Heracles
No, I have faith in your right hand, and only yours.   1115

Admetus
My lord, you are forcing me to act against my wish.

Heracles
Be brave. Reach out your hand and take the stranger's.

Admetus

                                    So.
Here is my hand; I feel like Perseus killing the
  gorgon.

Heracles
You have her?

Admetus
                Yes, I have her.

Heracles
                      Keep her, then. Some day
you will say the son of Zeus came as your generous
  guest.   1120
But look at her. See if she does not seem most like
your wife. Your grief is over now. Your luck is back.

Admetus
Gods, what shall I think! Amazement beyond hope,
  as I
look on this woman, this wife. Is she really mine,
or some sweet mockery for God to stun me with?   1125

55

Heracles
Not so. This is your own wife you see. She is here.

Admetus
Be careful she is not some phantom from the depths.

Heracles
The guest and friend you took was no necromancer.

Admetus
Do I see my wife, whom I was laying in the grave?

Heracles
Surely. But I do not wonder at your unbelief.   1130

Admetus
May I touch her, and speak to her, as my living wife?

Heracles
Speak to her. All that you desired is yours.

Admetus

                        Oh, eyes
and body of my dearest wife, I have you now
beyond all hope. I never thought to see you again.

Heracles
You have her. May no god hate you for your
   happiness.   1135

Admetus
O nobly sprung child of all-highest Zeus, may good
fortune go with you. May the father who gave you
   birth
keep you. You alone raised me up when I was down.
How did you bring her back from down there to the
   light?

Heracles
I fought a certain deity who had charge of her.   1140

Admetus
Where do you say you fought this match with Death?

56

Heracles

Beside
the tomb itself. I sprang and caught him in my
hands.

Admetus
But why is my wife standing here, and does not
speak?

Heracles
You are not allowed to hear her speak to you until
her obligations to the gods who live below   1145
are washed away. Until the third morning comes.
So now
take her and lead her inside, and for the rest of time,
Admetus, be just. Treat your guests as they deserve.
And now goodbye. I have my work that I must do,
and go to face the lordly son of Sthenelus.   1150

Admetus
No, stay with us and be the guest of our hearth.

Heracles

There still
will be a time for that, but I must press on now.

Admetus
Success go with you. May you find your way back
here.

(*Heracles goes.*)

I proclaim to all the people of my tetrarchy
that, for these blessed happenings, they shall set up
dances, and the altars smoke with sacrifice offered.   1155
For now we shall make our life again, and it will be
a better one.
I was lucky. That I cannot deny.

(*He takes Alcestis by the hand and leads
her inside the house.*)

Chorus (going)
Many are the forms of what is unknown.
Much that the gods achieve is surprise.   1160
What we look for does not come to pass;
God finds a way for what none foresaw.
Such was the end of this story.

THE MEDEA

Translated by Rex Warner

INTRODUCTION TO *THE MEDEA*

THE Athenian audience who saw the first performance of Euripides' *Medea* at the state dramatic contest in 431 B.C. and who awarded the third prize to Euripides would have been familiar with the whole story of the chief characters, and we, twenty-three centuries later, are handicapped in our understanding of the play if we have not at least some knowledge of the same story.

The Athenians would have known Medea as a barbarian princess and as a sorceress, related to the gods. She came from the faraway land of Colchis at the eastern extremity of the Black Sea, where her father, King Aeetes, a sorcerer himself and the son of Helius, god of the sun, kept the Golden Fleece. Here Jason had come with the Argonauts, the first expedition of western Greeks against the eastern barbarians. Medea had fallen in love with him, and by her aid he was able to avoid the traps laid for him by Aeetes, to regain the Golden Fleece, and to escape, taking Medea with him. She, to assist the escape, had murdered her own brother, strewing the pieces of his body over the water so that her father's fleet, while collecting the fragments for burial, might lose time in the pursuit of the fugitives.

Medea and Jason then settled in Jason's hereditary kingdom of Iolcus, where Pelias, his uncle, still cheated him of his rights. Medea, hoping to do Jason a favor, persuaded the daughters of Pelias to attempt, under her guidance, a magic rejuvenation of their father. The old man was to be killed, cut in pieces, and then, with the aid of herbs and incantations, restored to his first youth. The unsuspecting daughters did as they were told, and Medea left them with their father's blood upon their hands. However, the result of this crime was no advancement for Jason but rather exile for him, Medea, and their two children.

From Iolcus they came to Corinth, the scene of Euripides' play. Here Jason, either, as he says himself, wishing to strengthen his own economic position, or, as Medea thinks, because he was tired of his dangerous foreign wife, put her aside and married the daughter of Creon, king of Corinth. It is at this point that the action of the play begins; but the Athenian audience would know well enough what the plot would be. They would know that Medea, in her jealous rage, would destroy both Creon and his daughter by means of a poisoned robe which clung to the flesh and burned it; that, despairing of her children's safety and wishing through them to injure Jason in every way, she would kill them with her own hands; and that, finally, by supernatural means, she would escape to their own city and take refuge with the old King Aegeus.

CHARACTERS

Medea, princess of Colchis and wife of

Jason, son of Aeson, king of Iolcus

Two children of Medea and Jason

Creon, king of Corinth

Aegeus, king of Athens

Nurse to Medea

Tutor to Medea's children

Messenger

Chorus of Corinthian Women

THE MEDEA

SCENE: *In front of Medea's house in Corinth. Enter from the house Medea's nurse.*

Nurse
How I wish the Argo never had reached the land
Of Colchis, skimming through the blue Symplegades,
Nor ever had fallen in the glades of Pelion
The smitten fir-tree to furnish oars for the hands
Of heroes who in Pelias' name attempted   5
The Golden Fleece! For then my mistress Medea
Would not have sailed for the towers of the land of
    Iolcus,
Her heart on fire with passionate love for Jason;
Nor would she have persuaded the daughters of Pelias
To kill their father, and now be living here   10
In Corinth with her husband and children. She gave
Pleasure to the people of her land of exile,
And she herself helped Jason in every way.
This is indeed the greatest salvation of all—
For the wife not to stand apart from the husband.   15
But now there's hatred everywhere, Love is diseased.
For, deserting his own children and my mistress,
Jason has taken a royal wife to his bed,
The daughter of the ruler of this land, Creon.
And poor Medea is slighted, and cries aloud on the   20
Vows they made to each other, the right hands
    clasped
In eternal promise. She calls upon the gods to witness
What sort of return Jason has made to her love.
She lies without food and gives herself up to suffering,

63

Wasting away every moment of the day in tears.   25
So it has gone since she knew herself slighted by him.
Not stirring an eye, not moving her face from the
  ground,
No more than either a rock or surging sea water
She listens when she is given friendly advice.
Except that sometimes she twists back her white
  neck and   30
Moans to herself, calling out on her father's name,
And her land, and her home betrayed when she came
  away with
A man who now is determined to dishonor her.
Poor creature, she has discovered by her sufferings
What it means to one not to have lost one's own
  country.   35
She has turned from the children and does not like to
  see them.
I am afraid she may think of some dreadful thing,
For her heart is violent. She will never put up with
The treatment she is getting. I know and fear her
Lest she may sharpen a sword and thrust to the heart, 40
Stealing into the palace where the bed is made,
Or even kill the king and the new-wedded groom,
And thus bring a greater misfortune on herself.
She's a strange woman. I know it won't be easy
To make an enemy of her and come off best.   45
But here the children come. They have finished
  playing.
They have no thought at all of their mother's trouble.
Indeed it is not usual for the young to grieve.

(*Enter from the right the slave who is the tutor
  to Medea's two small children. The
  children follow him.*)

Tutor

You old retainer of my mistress' household,
Why are you standing here all alone in front of the   50

64

Gates and moaning to yourself over your misfortune?
Medea could not wish you to leave her alone.

Nurse
Old man, and guardian of the children of Jason,
If one is a good servant, it's a terrible thing
When one's master's luck is out; it goes to one's heart.   55
So I myself have got into such a state of grief
That a longing stole over me to come outside here
And tell the earth and air of my mistress' sorrows.

Tutor
Has the poor lady not yet given up her crying?

Nurse
Given up? She's at the start, not halfway through her
    tears.   60

Tutor
Poor fool—if I may call my mistress such a name—
How ignorant she is of trouble more to come.

Nurse
What do you mean, old man? You needn't fear to
    speak.

Tutor
Nothing. I take back the words which I used just
    now.

Nurse
Don't, by your beard, hide this from me, your fellow-
    servant.   65
If need be, I'll keep quiet about what you tell me.

Tutor
I heard a person saying, while I myself seemed
Not to be paying attention, when I was at the place
Where the old draught-players sit, by the holy
    fountain,
That Creon, ruler of the land, intends to drive   70

These children and their mother in exile from
  Corinth.
But whether what he said is really true or not
I do not know. I pray that it may not be true.

Nurse
And will Jason put up with it that his children
Should suffer so, though he's no friend to their
  mother?   75

Tutor
Old ties give place to new ones. As for Jason, he
No longer has a feeling for this house of ours.

Nurse
It's black indeed for us, when we add new to old
Sorrows before even the present sky has cleared.

Tutor
But you be silent, and keep all this to yourself.   80
It is not the right time to tell our mistress of it.

Nurse
Do you hear, children, what a father he is to you?
I wish he were dead—but no, he is still my master.
Yet certainly he has proved unkind to his dear ones.

Tutor
What's strange in that? Have you only just discovered   85
That everyone loves himself more than his neighbor?
Some have good reason, others get something out
  of it.
So Jason neglects his children for the new bride.

Nurse
Go indoors, children. That will be the best thing.
And you, keep them to themselves as much as
  possible.   90
Don't bring them near their mother in her angry
  mood.
For I've seen her already blazing her eyes at them

As though she meant some mischief and I am
  sure that
She'll not stop raging until she has struck at someone.
May it be an enemy and not a friend she hurts!   95

(*Medea is heard inside the house.*)

Medea
Ah, wretch! Ah, lost in my sufferings,
I wish, I wish I might die.

Nurse
What did I say, dear children? Your mother
Frets her heart and frets it to anger.
Run away quickly into the house,   100
And keep well out of her sight.
Don't go anywhere near, but be careful
Of the wildness and bitter nature
Of that proud mind.
Go now! Run quickly indoors.   105
It is clear that she soon will put lightning
In that cloud of her cries that is rising
With a passion increasing. O, what will she do,
Proud-hearted and not to be checked on her course,
A soul bitten into with wrong?   110

(*The Tutor takes the children into the house.*)

Medea
Ah, I have suffered
What should be wept for bitterly. I hate you,
Children of a hateful mother. I curse you
And your father. Let the whole house crash.

Nurse
Ah, I pity you, you poor creature.   115
How can your children share in their father's
Wickedness? Why do you hate them? Oh children,
How much I fear that something may happen!
Great people's tempers are terrible, always

Having their own way, seldom checked,   120
Dangerous they shift from mood to mood.
How much better to have been accustomed
To live on equal terms with one's neighbors.
I would like to be safe and grow old in a   125
Humble way. What is moderate sounds best,
Also in practice *is* best for everyone.
Greatness brings no profit to people.
God indeed, when in anger, brings
Greater ruin to great men's houses.   130

(*Enter, on the right, a Chorus of Corinthian women.
They have come to inquire about Medea
and to attempt to console her.*)

Chorus
I heard the voice, I heard the cry
Of Colchis' wretched daughter.
Tell me, mother, is she not yet
At rest? Within the double gates   135
Of the court I heard her cry. I am sorry
For the sorrow of this home. O, say, what has
    happened?

Nurse
There is no home. It's over and done with.   140
Her husband holds fast to his royal wedding,
While she, my mistress, cries out her eyes
There in her room, and takes no warmth from
Any word of any friend.

Medea
Oh, I wish
That lightning from heaven would split my head open.
Oh, what use have I now for life?   145
I would find my release in death
And leave hateful existence behind me.

Chorus
O God and Earth and Heaven!

Did you hear what a cry was that
Which the sad wife sings?   150
Poor foolish one, why should you long
For that appalling rest?
The final end of death comes fast.
No need to pray for that.
Suppose your man gives honor   155
To another woman's bed.
It often happens. Don't be hurt.
God will be your friend in this.
You must not waste away
Grieving too much for him who shared your bed.

Medea
Great Themis, lady Artemis, behold   160
The things I suffer, though I made him promise,
My hateful husband. I pray that I may see him,
Him and his bride and all their palace shattered
For the wrong they dare to do me without cause.   165
Oh, my father! Oh, my country! In what dishonor
I left you, killing my own brother for it.

Nurse
Do you hear what she says, and how she cries
On Themis, the goddess of Promises, and on Zeus,
Whom we believe to be the Keeper of Oaths?   170
Of this I am sure, that no small thing
Will appease my mistress' anger.

Chorus
Will she come into our presence?
Will she listen when we are speaking
To the words we say?   175
I wish she might relax her rage
And temper of her heart.
My willingness to help will never
Be wanting to my friends.
But go inside and bring her   180
Out of the house to us,

69

And speak kindly to her: hurry,
Before she wrongs her own.
This passion of hers moves to something great.

Nurse
I will, but I doubt if I'll manage
To win my mistress over.   185
But still I'll attempt it to please you.
Such a look she will flash on her servants
If any comes near with a message,
Like a lioness guarding her cubs.
It is right, I think, to consider   190
Both stupid and lacking in foresight
Those poets of old who wrote songs
For revels and dinners and banquets,
Pleasant sounds for men living at ease;
But none of them all has discovered   195
How to put to an end with their singing
Or musical instruments grief,
Bitter grief, from which death and disaster
Cheat the hopes of a house. Yet how good
If music could cure men of this! But why raise   200
To no purpose the voice at a banquet? For *there* is
Already abundance of pleasure for men
With a joy of its own.

(*The Nurse goes into the house.*)

Chorus
I heard a shriek that is laden with sorrow.
Shrilling out her hard grief she cries out   205
Upon him who betrayed both her bed and her
   marriage.
Wronged, she calls on the gods,
On the justice of Zeus, the oath sworn,
Which brought her away
To the opposite shore of the Greeks   210
Through the gloomy salt straits to the gateway
Of the salty unlimited sea.

70

THE MEDEA

*(Medea, attended by servants, comes
out of the house.)*

Medea

Women of Corinth, I have come outside to you
Lest you should be indignant with me; for I know   215
That many people are overproud, some when alone,
And others when in company. And those who live
Quietly, as I do, get a bad reputation.
For a just judgment is not evident in the eyes
When a man at first sight hates another, before   220
Learning his character, being in no way injured;
And a foreigner especially must adapt himself.
I'd not approve of even a fellow-countryman
Who by pride and want of manners offends his
  neighbors.
But on me this thing has fallen so unexpectedly,   225
It has broken my heart. I am finished. I let go
All my life's joy. My friends, I only want to die.
It was everything to me to think well of one man,
And he, my own husband, has turned out wholly vile.
Of all things which are living and can form a
  judgment   230
We women are the most unfortunate creatures.
Firstly, with an excess of wealth it is required
For us to buy a husband and take for our bodies
A master; for not to take one is even worse.
And now the question is serious whether we take   235
A good or bad one; for there is no easy escape
For a woman, nor can she say no to her marriage.
She arrives among new modes of behavior and
  manners,
And needs prophetic power, unless she has learned
  at home,
How best to manage him who shares the bed
  with her.   240
And if we work out all this well and carefully,

And the husband lives with us and lightly bears his
    yoke,
Then life is enviable. If not, I'd rather die.
A man, when he's tired of the company in his home,
Goes out of the house and puts an end to his boredom   245
And turns to a friend or companion of his own age.
But we are forced to keep our eyes on one alone.
What they say of us is that we have a peaceful time
Living at home, while they do the fighting in war.
How wrong they are! I would very much rather stand   250
Three times in the front of battle than bear one child.
Yet what applies to me does not apply to you.
You have a country. Your family home is here.
You enjoy life and the company of your friends.
But I am deserted, a refugee, thought nothing of   255
By my husband—something he won in a foreign land.
I have no mother or brother, nor any relation
With whom I can take refuge in this sea of woe.
This much then is the service I would beg from you.
If I can find the means or devise any scheme   260
To pay my husband back for what he has done
    to me—
Him and his father-in-law and the girl who married
    him—
Just to keep silent. For in other ways a woman
Is full of fear, defenseless, dreads the sight of cold
Steel; but, when once she is wronged in the matter
    of love,   265
No other soul can hold so many thoughts of blood.

Chorus
This I will promise. You are in the right, Medea,
In paying your husband back. I am not surprised
    at you
For being sad.
            But look! I see our King Creon
Approaching. He will tell us of some new plan.   270

    (*Enter, from the right, Creon, with attendants.*)

Creon

You, with that angry look, so set against your husband,
Medea, I order you to leave my territories
An exile, and take along with you your two children,
And not to waste time doing it. It is my decree,
And I will see it done. I will not return home   275
Until you are cast from the boundaries of my land.

Medea

Oh, this is the end for me. I am utterly lost.
Now I am in the full force of the storm of hate
And have no harbor from ruin to reach easily.
Yet still, in spite of it all, I'll ask the question: 280
What is your reason, Creon, for banishing me?

Creon

I am afraid of you—why should I dissemble it?—
Afraid that you may injure my daughter mortally.
Many things accumulate to support my feeling.
You are a clever woman, versed in evil arts,   285
And are angry at having lost your husband's love.
I hear that you are threatening, so they tell me,
To do something against my daughter and Jason
And me, too. I shall take my precautions first.
I tell you, I prefer to earn your hatred now   290
Than to be soft-hearted and afterward regret it.

Medea

This is not the first time, Creon. Often previously
Through being considered clever I have suffered
    much.
A person of sense ought never to have his children
Brought up to be more clever than the average.   295
For, apart from cleverness bringing them no profit,
It will make them objects of envy and ill-will.
If you put new ideas before the eyes of fools
They'll think you foolish and worthless into the
    bargain;

73

And if you are thought superior to those who have   300
Some reputation for learning, you will become hated.
I have some knowledge myself of how this happens;
For being clever, I find that some will envy me,
Others object to me. Yet all my cleverness
Is not so much.   305

               Well, then, are you frightened, Creon,
That I should harm you? There is no need. It is not
My way to transgress the authority of a king.
How have you injured me? You gave your daughter away
To the man you wanted. Oh, certainly I hate   310
My husband, but you, I think, have acted wisely;
Nor do I grudge it you that your affairs go well.
May the marriage be a lucky one! Only let me
Live in this land. For even though I have been wronged,
I will not raise my voice, but submit to my betters.   315

Creon

What you say sounds gentle enough. Still in my heart
I greatly dread that you are plotting some evil,
And therefore I trust you even less than before.
A sharp-tempered woman, or, for that matter, a man,
Is easier to deal with than the clever type   320
Who holds her tongue. No. You must go. No need for more
Speeches. The thing is fixed. By no manner of means
Shall you, an enemy of mine, stay in my country.

Medea

I beg you. By your knees, by your new-wedded girl.

Creon

Your words are wasted. You will never persuade me.   325

Medea

Will you drive me out, and give no heed to my prayers?

Creon
I will, for I love my family more than you.

Medea
O my country! How bitterly now I remember you!

Creon
I love my country too—next after my children.

Medea
Oh what an evil to men is passionate love!   330

Creon
That would depend on the luck that goes along with it.

Medea
O God, do not forget who is the cause of this!

Creon
Go. It is no use. Spare me the pain of forcing you.

Medea
I'm spared no pain. I lack no pain to be spared me.

Creon
Then you'll be removed by force by one of my men.   335

Medea
No, Creon, not that! But do listen, I beg you.

Creon
Woman, you seem to want to create a disturbance.

Medea
I *will* go into exile. *This* is not what I beg for.

Creon
Why then this violence and clinging to my hand?

Medea
Allow me to remain here just for this one day,   340
So I may consider where to live in my exile,
And look for support for my children, since their
   father

Chooses to make no kind of provision for them.
Have pity on them! You have children of your own.
It is natural for you to look kindly on them. 345
For myself I do not mind if I go into exile.
It is the children being in trouble that I mind.

Creon

There is nothing tyrannical about my nature,
And by showing mercy I have often been the loser.
Even now I know that I am making a mistake. 350
All the same you shall have your will. But this I
    tell you,
That if the light of heaven tomorrow shall see you,
You and your children in the confines of my land,
You die. This word I have spoken is firmly fixed.
But now, if you must stay, stay for this day alone. 355
For in it you can do none of the things I fear.

(*Exit Creon with his attendants.*)

Chorus

Oh, unfortunate one! Oh, cruel!
Where will you turn? Who will help you?
What house or what land to preserve you 360
From ill can you find?
Medea, a god has thrown suffering
Upon you in waves of despair.

Medea

Things have gone badly every way. No doubt of that
But not these things this far, and don't imagine so. 365
There are still trials to come for the new-wedded pair,
And for their relations pain that will mean something.
Do you think that I would ever have fawned on that
    man
Unless I had some end to gain or profit in it?
I would not even have spoken or touched him with
    my hands. 370
But he has got to such a pitch of foolishness

76

That, though he could have made nothing of all my
    plans
By exiling me, he has given me this one day
To stay here, and in this I will make dead bodies
Of three of my enemies—father, the girl, and my
    husband.   375
I have many ways of death which I might suit to
    them,
And do not know, friends, which one to take in hand;
Whether to set fire underneath their bridal mansion,
Or sharpen a sword and thrust it to the heart,
Stealing into the palace where the bed is made.   380
There is just one obstacle to this. If I am caught
Breaking into the house and scheming against it,
I shall die, and give my enemies cause for laughter.
It is best to go by the straight road, the one in which
I am most skilled, and make away with them by
    poison.   385
So be it then.
And now suppose them dead. What town will receive
    me?
What friend will offer me a refuge in his land,
Or the guaranty of his house and save my own life?
There is none. So I must wait a little time yet,
And if some sure defense should then appear for me,   390
In craft and silence I will set about this murder.
But if my fate should drive me on without help,
Even though death is certain, I will take the sword
Myself and kill, and steadfastly advance to crime.
It shall not be—I swear it by her, my mistress,   395
Whom most I honor and have chosen as partner,
Hecate, who dwells in the recesses of my hearth—
That any man shall be glad to have injured me.
Bitter I will make their marriage for them and
    mournful,
Bitter the alliance and the driving me out of the land.   400
Ah, come, Medea, in your plotting and scheming

Leave nothing untried of all those things which you
    know.
Go forward to the dreadful act. The test has come
For resolution. You see how you are treated. Never
Shall you be mocked by Jason's Corinthian wedding,   405
Whose father was noble, whose grandfather Helius.
You have the skill. What is more, you were born a
    woman,
And women, though most helpless in doing good
    deeds,
Are of every evil the cleverest of contrivers.

Chorus
Flow backward to your sources, sacred rivers,   410
And let the world's great order be reversed.
It is the thoughts of *men* that are deceitful,
Their pledges that are loose.   415
Story shall now turn my condition to a fair one,
Women are paid their due.
No more shall evil-sounding fame be theirs.   420

Cease now, you muses of the ancient singers,
To tell the tale of my unfaithfulness;
For not on us did Phoebus, lord of music,
Bestow the lyre's divine   425
Power, for otherwise I should have sung an answer
To the other sex. Long time
Has much to tell of us, and much of them.   430

You sailed away from your father's home,
With a heart on fire you passed
The double rocks of the sea.
And now in a foreign country   435
You have lost your rest in a widowed bed,
And are driven forth, a refugee
In dishonor from the land.

Good faith has gone, and no more remains
In great Greece a sense of shame.   440
It has flown away to the sky.

No father's house for a haven
Is at hand for you now, and another queen
Of your bed has dispossessed you and
Is mistress of your home.   445

(*Enter Jason, with attendants.*)

Jason
This is not the first occasion that I have noticed
How hopeless it is to deal with a stubborn temper.
For, with reasonable submission to our ruler's will,
You might have lived in this land and kept your
  home.
As it is you are going to be exiled for your loose
  speaking.   450
Not that I mind myself. You are free to continue
Telling everyone that Jason is a worthless man.
But as to your talk about the king, consider
Yourself most lucky that exile is your punishment.
I, for my part, have always tried to calm down   455
The anger of the king, and wished you to remain.
But you will not give up your folly, continually
Speaking ill of him, and so you are going to be
  banished.
All the same, and in spite of your conduct, I'll not
  desert
My friends, but have come to make some provision
  for you,   460
So that you and the children may not be penniless
Or in need of anything in exile. Certainly
Exile brings many troubles with it. And even
If you hate me, I cannot think badly of you.

Medea
O coward in every way—that is what I call you,   465
With bitterest reproach for your lack of manliness,
You have come, you, my worst enemy, have come
  to me!
It is not an example of overconfidence

Or of boldness thus to look your friends in the face,   470
Friends you have injured—no, it is the worst of all
Human diseases, shamelessness. But you did well
To come, for I can speak ill of you and lighten
My heart, and you will suffer while you are listening.
And first I will begin from what happened first.   475
I saved your life, and every Greek knows I saved it,
Who was a shipmate of yours aboard the Argo,
When you were sent to control the bulls that breathed
    fire
And yoke them, and when you would sow that deadly
    field.
Also that snake, who encircled with his many folds   480
The Golden Fleece and guarded it and never slept,
I killed, and so gave you the safety of the light.
And I myself betrayed my father and my home,
And came with you to Pelias' land of Iolcus.
And then, showing more willingness to help than
    wisdom,
    485
I killed him, Pelias, with a most dreadful death
At his own daughters' hands, and took away your fear.
This is how I behaved to you, you wretched man,
And you forsook me, took another bride to bed,
Though you had children; for, if that had not been,   490
You would have had an excuse for another wedding.
Faith in your word has gone. Indeed, I cannot tell
Whether you think the gods whose names you swore
    by then
Have ceased to rule and that new standards are
    set up,
Since you must know you have broken your word
    to me.
    495
O my right hand, and the knees which you often
    clasped
In supplication, how senselessly I am treated
By this bad man, and how my hopes have missed
    their mark!

Come, I will share my thoughts as though you were
    a friend—
You! Can I think that you would ever treat me well?   500
But I will do it, and these questions will make you
Appear the baser. Where am I to go? To my father's?
Him I betrayed and his land when I came with you.
To Pelias' wretched daughters? What a fine welcome
They would prepare for me who murdered their
    father!   505
For this is my position—hated by my friends
At home, I have, in kindness to you, made enemies
Of others whom there was no need to have injured.
And how happy among Greek women you have
    made me
On your side for all this! A distinguished husband   510
I have—for breaking promises. When in misery
I am cast out of the land and go into exile,
Quite without friends and all alone with my children,
That will be a fine shame for the new-wedded groom,
For his children to wander as beggars and she who
    saved him.   515
O God, you have given to mortals a sure method
Of telling the gold that is pure from the counterfeit;
Why is there no mark engraved upon men's bodies,
By which we could know the true ones from the
    false ones?

Chorus
It is a strange form of anger, difficult to cure,   520
When two friends turn upon each other in hatred.

Jason
As for me, it seems I must be no bad speaker.
But, like a man who has a good grip of the tiller,
Reef up his sail, and so run away from under
This mouthing tempest, woman, of your bitter tongue.   525
Since you insist on building up your kindness to me,
My view is that Cypris was alone responsible
Of men and gods for the preserving of my life.

You are clever enough—but really I need not enter
Into the story of how it was love's inescapable   530
Power that compelled you to keep my person safe.
On this I will not go into too much detail.
In so far as you helped me, you did well enough.
But on this question of saving me, I can prove
You have certainly got from me more than you gave.   535
Firstly, instead of living among barbarians,
You inhabit a Greek land and understand our ways,
How to live by law instead of the sweet will of force.
And all the Greeks considered you a clever woman.
You were honored for it; while, if you were living at   540
The ends of the earth, nobody would have heard
   of you.
For my part, rather than stores of gold in my house
Or power to sing even sweeter songs than Orpheus,
I'd choose the fate that made me a distinguished man.
There is my reply to your story of my labors.   545
Remember it was you who started the argument.
Next for your attack on my wedding with the
   princess:
Here I will prove that, first, it was a clever move,
Secondly, a wise one, and, finally, that I made it
In your best interests and the children's. Please keep
   calm.
                                                                 550
When I arrived here from the land of Iolcus,
Involved, as I was, in every kind of difficulty,
What luckier chance could I have come across than
   this,
An exile to marry the daughter of the king?
It was not—the point that seems to upset you—that I   555
Grew tired of your bed and felt the need of a new
   bride;
Nor with any wish to outdo your number of children.
We have enough already. I am quite content.
But—this was the main reason—that we might live
   well,
And not be short of anything. I know that all   560

A man's friends leave him stone-cold if he becomes
   poor.
Also that I might bring my children up worthily
Of my position, and, by producing more of them
To be brothers of yours, we would draw the families
Together and all be happy. You need no children.   565
And it pays me to do good to those I have now
By having others. Do you think this a bad plan?
You wouldn't if the love question hadn't upset you.
But you women have got into such a state of mind
That, if your life at night is good, you think you have   570
Everything; but, if in that quarter things go wrong,
You will consider your best and truest interests
Most hateful. It would have been better far for men
To have got their children in some other way, and
   women
Not to have existed. Then life would have been good.   575

Chorus
Jason, though you have made this speech of yours
   look well,
Still I think, even though others do not agree,
You have betrayed your wife and are acting badly.

Medea
Surely in many ways I hold different views
From others, for I think that the plausible speaker   580
Who is a villain deserves the greatest punishment.
Confident in his tongue's power to adorn evil,
He stops at nothing. Yet he is not really wise.
As in your case. There is no need to put on the airs
Of a clever speaker, for one word will lay you flat.   585
If you were not a coward, you would not have married
Behind my back, but discussed it with me first.

Jason
And you, no doubt, would have furthered the proposal,
If I had told you of it, you who even now
Are incapable of controlling your bitter temper.   590

Medea
It was not that. No, you thought it was not respectable
As you got on in years to have a foreign wife.

Jason
Make sure of this: it was not because of a woman
I made the royal alliance in which I now live,
But, as I said before, I wished to preserve you   595
And breed a royal progeny to be brothers
To the children I have now, a sure defense to us.

Medea
Let me have no happy fortune that brings pain
    with it,
Or prosperity which is upsetting to the mind!

Jason
Change your ideas of what you want, and show more
    sense.   600
Do not consider painful what is good for you,
Nor, when you are lucky, think yourself unfortunate.

Medea
You can insult me. You have somewhere to turn to.
But I shall go from this land into exile, friendless.

Jason
It was what you chose yourself. Don't blame others
    for it.   605

Medea
And how did I choose it? Did I betray my husband?

Jason
You called down wicked curses on the king's family.

Medea
A curse, that is what I am become to your house too.

Jason
I do not propose to go into all the rest of it;
But, if you wish for the children or for yourself   610

In exile to have some of my money to help you,
Say so, for I am prepared to give with open hand,
Or to provide you with introductions to my friends
Who will treat you well. You are a fool if you do not
Accept this. Cease your anger and you will profit.   615

Medea
I shall never accept the favors of friends of yours,
Nor take a thing from you, so you need not offer it.
There is no benefit in the gifts of a bad man.

Jason
Then, in any case, I call the gods to witness that
I wish to help you and the children in every way,   620
But you refuse what is good for you. Obstinately
You push away your friends. You are sure to suffer
    for it.

Medea
Go! No doubt you hanker for your virginal bride,
And are guilty of lingering too long out of her house.
Enjoy your wedding. But perhaps—with the help of
    God—   625
You will make the kind of marriage that you will
    regret.

                    (*Jason goes out with his attendants.*)

Chorus
When love is in excess
It brings a man no honor
Nor any worthiness.
But if in moderation Cypris comes,   630
There is no other power at all so gracious.
O goddess, never on me let loose the unerring
Shaft of your bow in the poison of desire.

Let my heart be wise   635
It is the gods' best gift.
On me let mighty Cypris

85

Inflict no wordy wars or restless anger
To urge my passion to a different love.
But with discernment may she guide women's wed-
    dings,   640
Honoring most what is peaceful in the bed.

O country and home,
Never, never may I be without you,
Living the hopeless life,   645
Hard to pass through and painful,
Most pitiable of all.
Let death first lay me low and death
Free me from this daylight.
There is no sorrow above   650
The loss of a native land.

I have seen it myself,
Do not tell of a secondhand story.
Neither city nor friend   655
Pitied you when you suffered
The worst of sufferings.
O let him die ungraced whose heart
Will not reward his friends,   660
Who cannot open an honest mind
No friend will he be of mine.

                (*Enter Aegeus, king of Athens, an*
                         old friend of Medea.)

Aegeus
Medea, greeting! This is the best introduction
Of which men know for conversation between friends.

Medea
Greeting to you too, Aegeus, son of King Pandion.   665
Where have you come from to visit this country's soil?

Aegeus
I have just left the ancient oracle of Phoebus.

Medea
And why did you go to earth's prophetic center?

Aegeus
I went to inquire how children might be born to me.

Medea
Is it so? Your life still up to this point is childless?   670

Aegeus
Yes. By the fate of some power we have no children.

Medea
Have you a wife, or is there none to share your bed?

Aegeus
There is. Yes, I am joined to my wife in marriage.

Medea
And what did Phoebus say to you about children?

Aegeus
Words too wise for a mere man to guess their
meaning.   675

Medea
It is proper for me to be told the god's reply?

Aegeus
It is. For sure what is needed is cleverness.

Medea
Then what was his message? Tell me, if I may hear.

Aegeus
I am not to loosen the hanging foot of the wine-
skin . . .

Medea
Until you have done something, or reached some
country?   680

Aegeus
Until I return again to my hearth and house.

Medea
And for what purpose have you journeyed to this
land?

Aegeus
There is a man called Pittheus, king of Troezen.

Medea
A son of Pelops, they say, a most righteous man.

Aegeus
With him I wish to discuss the reply of the god.   685

Medea
Yes. He is wise and experienced in such matters.

Aegeus
And to me also the dearest of all my spear-friends.

Medea
Well, I hope you have good luck, and achieve your will.

Aegeus
But why this downcast eye of yours, and this pale
cheek?

Medea
O Aegeus, my husband has been the worst of all to me.   690

Aegeus
What do you mean? Say clearly what has caused
this grief.

Medea
Jason wrongs me, though I have never injured him.

Aegeus
What has he done? Tell me about it in clearer words.

Medea
He has taken a wife to his house, supplanting me.

Aegeus
Surely he would not dare to do a thing like that.   695

Medea
Be sure he has. Once dear, I now am slighted by him.

Aegeus
Did he fall in love? Or is he tired of your love?

Medea
He was greatly in love, this traitor to his friends.

Aegeus
Then let him go, if, as you say, he is so bad.

Medea
A passionate love—for an alliance with the king.   700

Aegeus
And who gave him his wife? Tell me the rest of it.

Medea
It was Creon, he who rules this land of Corinth.

Aegeus
Indeed, Medea, your grief was understandable.

Medea
I am ruined. And there is more to come: I am
    banished.

Aegeus
Banished? By whom? Here you tell me of a new
    wrong.   705

Medea
Creon drives me an exile from the land of Corinth.

Aegeus
Does Jason consent? I cannot approve of this.

Medea
He pretends not to, but he will put up with it.
Ah, Aegeus, I beg and beseech you, by your beard
And by your knees I am making myself your
    suppliant,   710
Have pity on me, have pity on your poor friend,

89

And do not let me go into exile desolate,
But receive me in your land and at your very hearth.
So may your love, with God's help, lead to the bearing
Of children, and so may you yourself die happy.   715
You do not know what a chance you have come
    on here.
I will end your childlessness, and I will make you able
To beget children. The drugs I know can do this.

Aegeus

For many reasons, woman, I am anxious to do
This favor for you. First, for the sake of the gods,   720
And then for the birth of children which you promise,
For in that respect I am entirely at my wits' end.
But this is my position: if you reach my land,
I, being in my rights, will try to befriend you.
But this much I must warn you of beforehand: 725
I shall not agree to take you out of this country;
But if you by yourself can reach my house, then you
Shall stay there safely. To none will I give you up
But from this land you must make your escape
    yourself,
For I do not wish to incur blame from my friends.   730

Medea

It shall be so. But, if I might have a pledge from you
For this, then I would have from you all I desire.

Aegeus

Do you not trust me? What is it rankles with you?

Medea

I trust you, yes. But the house of Pelias hates me,
And so does Creon. If you are bound by this oath,   735
When they try to drag me from your land, you
    will not
Abandon me; but if our pact is only words,
With no oath to the gods, you will be lightly armed,
Unable to resist their summons. I am weak,

While they have wealth to help them and a royal
   house.   740

Aegeus
You show much foresight for such negotiations.
Well, if you will have it so, I will not refuse.
For, both on my side this will be the safest way
To have some excuse to put forward to your enemies,
And for you it is more certain. You may name
   the gods.   745

Medea
Swear by the plain of Earth, and Helius, father
Of my father, and name together all the gods . . .

Aegeus
That I will act or not act in what way? Speak.

Medea
That you yourself will never cast me from your land,
Nor, if any of my enemies should demand me,   750
Will you, in your life, willingly hand me over.

Aegeus
I swear by the Earth, by the holy light of Helius,
By all the gods, I will abide by this you say.

Medea
Enough. And, if you fail, what shall happen to you?

Aegeus
What comes to those who have no regard for heaven.   755

Medea
Go on your way. Farewell. For I am satisfied.
And I will reach your city as soon as I can,
Having done the deed I have to do and gained my end.

                           (*Aegeus goes out.*)

Chorus
May Hermes, god of travelers,
Escort you, Aegeus, to your home!   760

And may you have the things you wish
So eagerly; for you
Appear to me to be a generous man.

Medea
God, and God's daughter, justice, and light of Helius!
Now, friends, has come the time of my triumph over   765
My enemies, and now my foot is on the road.
Now I am confident they will pay the penalty.
For this man, Aegeus, has been like a harbor to me
In all my plans just where I was most distressed.
To him I can fasten the cable of my safety   770
When I have reached the town and fortress of Pallas.
And now I shall tell to you the whole of my plan.
Listen to these words that are not spoken idly.
I shall send one of my servants to find Jason
And request him to come once more into my sight.   775
And when he comes, the words I'll say will be soft
    ones.
I'll say that I agree with him, that I approve
The royal wedding he has made, betraying me.
I'll say it was profitable, an excellent idea.
But I shall beg that my children may remain here: 780
Not that I would leave in a country that hates me
Children of mine to feel their enemies' insults,
But that by a trick I may kill the king's daughter.
For I will send the children with gifts in their hands
To carry to the bride, so as not to be banished—   785
A finely woven dress and a golden diadem.
And if she takes them and wears them upon her skin
She and all who touch the girl will die in agony;
Such poison will I lay upon the gifts I send.
But there, however, I must leave that account paid.   790
I weep to think of what a deed I have to do
Next after that; for I shall kill my own children.
My children, there is none who can give them safety.
And when I have ruined the whole of Jason's house,
I shall leave the land and flee from the murder of my   795

Dear children, and I shall have done a dreadful deed.
For it is not bearable to be mocked by enemies.
So it must happen. What profit have I in life?
I have no land, no home, no refuge from my pain.
My mistake was made the time I left behind me   800
My father's house, and trusted the words of a Greek,
Who, with heaven's help, will pay me the price
    for that.
For those children he had from me he will never
See alive again, nor will he on his new bride
Beget another child, for she is to be forced   805
To die a most terrible death by these my poisons.
Let no one think me a weak one, feeble-spirited,
A stay-at-home, but rather just the opposite,
One who can hurt my enemies and help my friends;
For the lives of such persons are most remembered.   810

Chorus
Since you have shared the knowledge of your plan
    with us,
I both wish to help you and support the normal
Ways of mankind, and tell you not to do this thing.

Medea
I can do no other thing. It is understandable
For you to speak thus. You have not suffered as I have. 815

Chorus
But can you have the heart to kill your flesh and
    blood?

Medea
Yes, for this is the best way to wound my husband.

Chorus
And you, too. Of women you will be most unhappy.

Medea
So it must be. No compromise is possible.

(*She turns to the Nurse.*)

Go, you, at once, and tell Jason to come to me.   820
You I employ on all affairs of greatest trust.
Say nothing of these decisions which I have made,
If you love your mistress, if you were born a woman.

Chorus
From of old the children of Erechtheus are
Splendid, the sons of blessed gods. They dwell   825
In Athens' holy and unconquered land,
Where famous Wisdom feeds them and they pass
     gaily
Always through that most brilliant air where once,
     they say,   830
That golden Harmony gave birth to the nine
Pure Muses of Pieria.

And beside the sweet flow of Cephisus' stream,   835
Where Cypris sailed, they say, to draw the water,
And mild soft breezes breathed along her path,
And on her hair were flung the sweet-smelling
     garlands   840
Of flowers of roses by the Lovers, the companions
Of Wisdom, her escort, the helpers of men
In every kind of excellence.   845

How then can these holy rivers
Or this holy land love you,
Or the city find you a home,
You, who will kill your children,
You, not pure with the rest?   850
O think of the blow at your children
And think of the blood that you shed.
O, over and over I beg you,
By your knees I beg you do not
Be the murderess of your babes!   855

O where will you find the courage
Or the skill of hand and heart,
When you set yourself to attempt
A deed so dreadful to do?

How, when you look upon them, 860
Can you tearlessly hold the decision
For murder? You will not be able,
When your children fall down and implore you,
You will not be able to dip
Steadfast your hand in their blood. 865

(*Enter Jason with attendants.*)

Jason
I have come at your request. Indeed, although you are
Bitter against me, this you shall have: I will listen
To what new thing you want, woman, to get from me.

Medea
Jason, I beg you to be forgiving toward me
For what I said. It is natural for you to bear with 870
My temper, since we have had much love together.
I have talked with myself about this and I have
Reproached myself. "Fool," I said, "why am I so mad?
Why am I set against those who have planned wisely?
Why make myself an enemy of the authorities 875
And of my husband, who does the best thing for me
By marrying royalty and having children who
Will be as brothers to my own? What is wrong
  with me?
Let me give up anger, for the gods are kind to me.
Have I not children, and do I not know that we 880
In exile from our country must be short of friends?"
When I considered this I saw that I had shown
Great lack of sense, and that my anger was foolish.
Now I agree with you. I think that you are wise
In having this other wife as well as me, and I 885
Was mad. I should have helped you in these plans
  of yours,
Have joined in the wedding, stood by the marriage
  bed,
Have taken pleasure in attendance on your bride.
But we women are what we are—perhaps a little

95

Worthless; and you men must not be like us in this,   890
Nor be foolish in return when we are foolish.
Now, I give in, and admit that then I was wrong.
I have come to a better understanding now.

(*She turns toward the house.*)

Children, come here, my children, come outdoors
   to us!
Welcome your father with me, and say goodbye to him,   895
And with your mother, who just now was his enemy,
Join again in making friends with him who loves us.

(*Enter the children, attended by the Tutor.*)

We have made peace, and all our anger is over.
Take hold of his right hand—O God, I am thinking
Of something which may happen in the secret future.   900
O children, will you just so, after a long life,
Hold out your loving arms at the grave? O children,
How ready to cry I am, how full of foreboding!
I am ending at last this quarrel with your father,
And look, my soft eyes have suddenly filled with tears.   905

Chorus
And the pale tears have started also in my eyes.
O may the trouble not grow worse than now it is!

Jason
I approve of what you say. And I cannot blame you
Even for what you said before. It is natural
For a woman to be wild with her husband when he   910
Goes in for secret love. But now your mind has
   turned
To better reasoning. In the end you have come to
The right decision, like the clever woman you are.
And of you, children, your father is taking care.
He has made, with God's help, ample provision
   for you.   915
For I think that a time will come when you will be
The leading people in Corinth with your brothers.

You must grow up. As to the future, your father
And those of the gods who love him will deal with
    that.
I want to see you, when you have become young men,   920
Healthy and strong, better men than my enemies.
Medea, why are your eyes all wet with pale tears?
Why is your cheek so white and turned away
    from me?
Are not these words of mine pleasing for you to hear?

Medea

It is nothing. I was thinking about these children.   925

Jason

You must be cheerful. I shall look after them well.

Medea

I will be. It is not that I distrust your words,
But a woman is a frail thing, prone to crying.

Jason

But why then should you grieve so much for these
    children?

Medea

I am their mother. When you prayed that they
    might live   930
I felt unhappy to think that these things will be.
But come, I have said something of the things I meant
To say to you, and now I will tell you the rest.
Since it is the king's will to banish me from here—
And for me, too, I know that this is the best thing,   935
Not to be in your way by living here or in
The king's way, since they think me ill-disposed
    to them—
I then am going into exile from this land;
But do you, so that you may have the care of them,
Beg Creon that the children may not be banished.   940

Jason

I doubt if I'll succeed, but still I'll attempt it.

Medea

Then you must tell your wife to beg from her father
That the children may be reprieved from banishment.

Jason

I will, and with her I shall certainly succeed.

Medea

If she is like the rest of us women, you will.   945
And I, too, will take a hand with you in this business,
For I will send her some gifts which are far fairer,
I am sure of it, than those which now are in fashion,
A finely woven dress and a golden diadem,
And the children shall present them. Quick, let one
    of you   950
Servants bring here to me that beautiful dress.

(One of her attendants goes into the house.)

She will be happy not in one way, but in a hundred,
Having so fine a man as you to share her bed,
And with this beautiful dress which Helius of old,
My father's father, bestowed on his descendants.   955

*(Enter attendant carrying the poisoned
dress and diadem.)*

There, children, take these wedding presents in your
    hands.
Take them to the royal princess, the happy bride,
And give them to her. She will not think little
    of them.

Jason

No, don't be foolish, and empty your hands of these.
Do you think the palace is short of dresses to wear?   960
Do you think there is no gold there? Keep them, don't
    give them
Away. If my wife considers me of any value,
She will think more of me than money, I am sure
    of it.

Medea

No, let me have my way. They say the gods themselves
Are moved by gifts, and gold does more with men
   than words.   965
Hers is the luck, her fortune that which god blesses;
She is young and a princess; but for my children's
   reprieve
I would give my very life, and not gold only.
Go children, go together to that rich palace,
Be suppliants to the new wife of your father,   970
My lady, beg her not to let you be banished.
And give her the dress--for this is of great importance,
That she should take the gift into her hand from yours.
Go, quick as you can. And bring your mother good
   news
By your success of those things which she longs
   to gain.   975

   (*Jason goes out with his attendants, followed by
        the Tutor and the children carrying
           the poisoned gifts.*)*

Chorus

Now there is no hope left for the children's lives.
Now there is none. They are walking already to
   murder.
The bride, poor bride, will accept the curse of the
   gold,
Will accept the bright diadem.
Around her yellow hair she will set that dress   980
Of death with her own hands.

The grace and the perfume and glow of the golden
   robe
Will charm her to put them upon her and wear the
   wreath,
And now her wedding will be with the dead below,   985
Into such a trap she will fall,

Poor thing, into such a fate of death and never
Escape from under that curse.

You, too, O wretched bridegroom, making your match
   with kings,   990
You do not see that you bring
Destruction on your children and on her,
Your wife, a fearful death.
Poor soul, what a fall is yours!   995

In your grief, too, I weep, mother of little children,
You who will murder your own,
In vengeance for the loss of married love
Which Jason has betrayed   1000
As he lives with another wife.

(Enter the Tutor with the children.)

Tutor
Mistress, I tell you that these children are reprieved,
And the royal bride has been pleased to take in her
   hands
Your gifts. In that quarter the children are secure.
But come,
Why do you stand confused when you are fortunate?   1005
Why have you turned round with your cheek away
   from me?
Are not these words of mine pleasing for you to hear?

Medea
Oh! I am lost!

Tutor
That word is not in harmony with my tidings.

Medea
I am lost, I am lost!

Tutor
        Am I in ignorance telling you
Of some disaster, and not the good news I thought?   1010

Medea
You have told what you have told. I do not blame you.

Tutor
Why then this downcast eye, and this weeping of
  tears?

Medea
Oh, I am forced to weep, old man. The gods and I,
I in a kind of madness, have contrived all this.

Tutor
Courage! You, too, will be brought home by your
  children.   1015

Medea
Ah, before that happens I shall bring others home.

Tutor
Others before you have been parted from their
  children.
Mortals must bear in resignation their ill luck.

Medea
That is what I shall do. But go inside the house,
And do for the children your usual daily work.   1020

> (*The Tutor goes into the house. Medea
>   turns to her children.*)

O children, O my children, you have a city,
You have a home, and you can leave me behind you,
And without your mother you may live there forever.
But I am going in exile to another land
Before I have seen you happy and taken pleasure
  in you,   1025
Before I have dressed your brides and made your
  marriage beds
And held up the torch at the ceremony of wedding.
Oh, what a wretch I am in this my self-willed
  thought!

What was the purpose, children, for which I reared
  you?
For all my travail and wearing myself away? 1030
They were sterile, those pains I had in the bearing
  of you.
Oh surely once the hopes in you I had, poor me,
Were high ones: you would look after me in old age,
And when I died would deck me well with your own
  hands;
A thing which all would have done. Oh but now it
  is gone, 1035
That lovely thought. For, once I am left without you,
Sad will be the life I'll lead and sorrowful for me.
And you will never see your mother again with
Your dear eyes, gone to another mode of living.
Why, children, do you look upon me with your eyes? 1040
Why do you smile so sweetly that last smile of all?
Oh, Oh, what can I do? My spirit has gone from me,
Friends, when I saw that bright look in the children's
  eyes.
I cannot bear to do it. I renounce my plans
I had before. I'll take my children away from 1045
This land. Why should I hurt their father with
  the pain
They feel, and suffer twice as much of pain myself?
No, no, I will not do it. I renounce my plans.
Ah, what is wrong with me? Do I want to let go
My enemies unhurt and be laughed at for it? 1050
I must face this thing. Oh, but what a weak woman
Even to admit to my mind these soft arguments.
Children, go into the house. And he whom law forbids
To stand in attendance at my sacrifices,
Let him see to it. I shall not mar my handiwork. 1055
Oh! Oh!
Do not, O my heart, you must not do these things!
Poor heart, let them go, have pity upon the children.
If they live with you in Athens they will cheer you.
No! By Hell's avenging furies it shall not be—

This shall never be, that I should suffer my children   1060
To be the prey of my enemies' insolence.
Every way is it fixed. The bride will not escape.
No, the diadem is now upon her head, and she,   1065
The royal princess, is dying in the dress, I know it.
But—for it is the most dreadful of roads for me
To tread, and them I shall send on a more dreadful
    still—
I wish to speak to the children.

(She calls the children to her.)

                Come, children, give
Me your hands, give your mother your hands to
    kiss them.   1070
Oh the dear hands, and O how dear are these lips
    to me,
And the generous eyes and the bearing of my children!
I wish you happiness, but not here in this world.
What is here your father took. Oh how good to
    hold you!
How delicate the skin, how sweet the breath of
    children!   1075
Go, go! I am no longer able, no longer
To look upon you. I am overcome by sorrow.

(The children go into the house.)

I know indeed what evil I intend to do,
But stronger than all my afterthoughts is my fury,
Fury that brings upon mortals the greatest evils.   1080

(She goes out to the right, toward the royal palace.)

Chorus
Often before
I have gone through more subtle reasons,
And have come upon questionings greater
Than a woman should strive to search out.
But we too have a goddess to help us   1085
And accompany us into wisdom.

Not all of us. Still you will find
Among many women a few,
And our sex is not without learning.
This I say, that those who have never   1090
Had children, who know nothing of it,
In happiness have the advantage
Over those who are parents.
The childless, who never discover
Whether children turn out as a good thing   1095
Or as something to cause pain, are spared
Many troubles in lacking this knowledge.
And those who have in their homes
The sweet presence of children, I see that their lives
Are all wasted away by their worries.   1100
First they must think how to bring them up well and
How to leave them something to live on.
And then after this whether all their toil
Is for those who will turn out good or bad,
Is still an unanswered question.
And of one more trouble, the last of all,   1105
That is common to mortals I tell.
For suppose you have found them enough for their
     living,
Suppose that the children have grown into youth
And have turned out good, still, if God so wills it,
Death will away with your children's bodies,
And carry them off into Hades.   1110
What is our profit, then, that for the sake of
Children the gods should pile upon mortals
After all else
This most terrible grief of all?   1115

(*Enter Medea, from the spectators' right.*)

Medea

Friends, I can tell you that for long I have waited
For the event. I stare toward the place from where
The news will come. And now, see one of Jason's
     servants

Is on his way here, and that labored breath of his
Shows he has tidings for us, and evil tidings.   1120

(*Enter, also from the right, the Messenger.*)

Messenger
Medea, you who have done such a dreadful thing,
So outrageous, run for your life, take what you can,
A ship to bear you hence or chariot on land.

Medea
And what is the reason deserves such flight as this?

Messenger
She is dead, only just now, the royal princess,   1125
And Creon dead, too, her father, by your poisons.

Medea
The finest words you have spoken. Now and hereafter
I shall count you among my benefactors and friends.

Messenger
What! Are you right in the mind? Are you not mad,
Woman? The house of the king is outraged by you.   1130
Do you enjoy it? Not afraid of such doings?

Medea
To what you say I on my side have something too
To say in answer. Do not be in a hurry, friend,
But speak. How did they die? You will delight me
    twice
As much again if you say they died in agony.   1135

Messenger
When those two children, born of you, had entered in,
Their father with them, and passed into the bride's
    house,
We were pleased, we slaves who were distressed by
    your wrongs.
All through the house we were talking of but one
    thing,

How you and your husband had made up your
    quarrel.   1140
Some kissed the children's hands and some their
    yellow hair,
And I myself was so full of my joy that I
Followed the children into the women's quarters.
Our mistress, whom we honor now instead of you,
Before she noticed that your two children were there,   1145
Was keeping her eye fixed eagerly on Jason.
Afterwards, however, she covered up her eyes,
Her cheek paled, and she turned herself away from
    him,
So disgusted was she at the children's coming there.
But your husband tried to end the girl's bad temper,   1150
And said, "You must not look unkindly on your
    friends.
Cease to be angry. Turn your head to me again.
Have as your friends the same ones as your husband
    has.
And take these gifts, and beg your father to reprieve
These children from their exile. Do it for my sake."   1155
She, when she saw the dress, could not restrain
    herself.
She agreed with all her husband said, and before
He and the children had gone far from the palace,
She took the gorgeous robe and dressed herself in it,
And put the golden crown around her curly locks,   1160
And arranged the set of the hair in a shining mirror,
And smiled at the lifeless image of herself in it.
Then she rose from her chair and walked about the
    room,
With her gleaming feet stepping most soft and
    delicate,
All overjoyed with the present. Often and often   1165
She would stretch her foot out straight and look
    along it.
But after that it was a fearful thing to see.

The color of her face changed, and she staggered
  back,
She ran, and her legs trembled, and she only just
Managed to reach a chair without falling flat down.   1170
An aged woman servant who, I take it, thought
This was some seizure of Pan or another god,
Cried out "God bless us," but that was before she saw
The white foam breaking through her lips and her
  rolling
The pupils of her eyes and her face all bloodless.   1175
Then she raised a different cry from that "God
  bless us,"
A huge shriek, and the women ran, one to the king,
One to the newly wedded husband to tell him
What had happened to his bride; and with frequent
  sound
The whole of the palace rang as they went running.   1180
One walking quickly round the course of a race-track
Would now have turned the bend and be close to
  the goal,
When she, poor girl, opened her shut and speechless
  eye,
And with a terrible groan she came to herself.
For a twofold pain was moving up against her.   1185
The wreath of gold that was resting around her head
Let forth a fearful stream of all-devouring fire,
And the finely woven dress your children gave to her
Was fastening on the unhappy girl's fine flesh.
She leapt up from the chair, and all on fire she ran,   1190
Shaking her hair now this way and now that, trying
To hurl the diadem away; but fixedly
The gold preserved its grip, and, when she shook her
  hair,
Then more and twice as fiercely the fire blazed out.
Till, beaten by her fate, she fell down to the ground,   1195
Hard to be recognized except by a parent.
Neither the setting of her eyes was plain to see,
Nor the shapeliness of her face. From the top of

Her head there oozed out blood and fire mixed together.
Like the drops on pine-bark, so the flesh from her bones
Dropped away, torn by the hidden fang of the poison. 1200
It was a fearful sight; and terror held us all
From touching the corpse. We had learned from what had happened.
But her wretched father, knowing nothing of the event,
Came suddenly to the house, and fell upon the corpse, 1205
And at once cried out and folded his arms about her,
And kissed her and spoke to her, saying, "O my poor child,
What heavenly power has so shamefully destroyed you?
And who has set me here like an ancient sepulcher,
Deprived of you? O let me die with you, my child!" 1210
And when he had made an end of his wailing and crying,
Then the old man wished to raise himself to his feet;
But, as the ivy clings to the twigs of the laurel,
So he stuck to the fine dress, and he struggled fearfully.
For he was trying to lift himself to his knee, 1215
And she was pulling him down, and when he tugged hard
He would be ripping his aged flesh from his bones.
At last his life was quenched, and the unhappy man
Gave up the ghost, no longer could hold up his head.
There they lie close, the daughter and the old father, 1220
Dead bodies, an event he prayed for in his tears.
As for your interests, I will say nothing of them,
For you will find your own escape from punishment.
Our human life I think and have thought a shadow,
And I do not fear to say that those who are held 1225
Wise among men and who search the reasons of things
Are those who bring the most sorrow on themselves.

For of mortals there is no one who is happy.
If wealth flows in upon one, one may be perhaps
Luckier than one's neighbor, but still not happy.   1230

(*Exit.*)

Chorus
Heaven, it seems, on this day has fastened many
Evils on Jason, and Jason has deserved them.
Poor girl, the daughter of Creon, how I pity you
And your misfortunes, you who have gone quite away
To the house of Hades because of marrying Jason.   1235

Medea
Women, my task is fixed: as quickly as I may
To kill my children, and start away from this land,
And not, by wasting time, to suffer my children
To be slain by another hand less kindly to them.
Force every way will have it they must die, and since   1240
This must be so. then I, their mother, shall kill them.
Oh, arm yourself in steel, my heart! Do not hang back
From doing this fearful and necessary wrong.
Oh, come, my hand, poor wretched hand, and take
    the sword,
Take it, step forward to this bitter starting point,   1245
And do not be a coward, do not think of them,
How sweet they are, and how you are their mother.
    Just for
This one short day be forgetful of your children,
Afterward weep; for even though you will kill them,
They were very dear—Oh, I am an unhappy woman!   1250

(*With a cry she rushes into the house.*)

Chorus
O Earth, and the far shining
Ray of the Sun, look down, look down upon
This poor lost woman, look, before she raises
The hand of murder against her flesh and blood.
Yours was the golden birth from which   1255

She sprang, and now I fear divine
Blood may be shed by men.
O heavenly light, hold back her hand,
Check her, and drive from out the house
The bloody Fury raised by fiends of Hell.   1260

Vain waste, your care of children;
Was it in vain you bore the babes you loved,
After you passed the inhospitable strait
Between the dark blue rocks, Symplegades?
O wretched one, how has it come,   1265
This heavy anger on your heart,
This cruel bloody mind?
For God from mortals asks a stern
Price for the stain of kindred blood
In like disaster falling on their homes.   1270

(A cry from one of the children is heard.)

Chorus
Do you hear the cry, do you hear the children's cry?
O you hard heart, O woman fated for evil!

One of the children (from within)
What can I do and how escape my mother's hands?

Another child (from within)
O my dear brother, I cannot tell. We are lost.

Chorus
Shall I enter the house? Oh, surely I should   1275
Defend the children from murder.

A child (from within)
O help us, in God's name, for now we need your help.
Now, now we are close to it. We are trapped by the
    sword.

Chorus
O your heart must have been made of rock or steel,
You who can kill   1280

With your own hand the fruit of your own womb.
Of one alone I have heard, one woman alone
Of those of old who laid her hands on her children,
Ino, sent mad by heaven when the wife of Zeus
Drove her out from her home and made her wander;   1285
And because of the wicked shedding of blood
Of her own children she threw
Herself, poor wretch, into the sea and stepped away
Over the sea-cliff to die with her two children.
What horror more can be? O women's love,   1290
So full of trouble,
How many evils have you caused already!

(*Enter Jason, with attendants.*)

Jason
You women, standing close in front of this dwelling,
Is she, Medea, she who did this dreadful deed,
Still in the house, or has she run away in flight?   1295
For she will have to hide herself beneath the earth,
Or raise herself on wings into the height of air,
If she wishes to escape the royal vengeance.
Does she imagine that, having killed our rulers,
She will herself escape uninjured from this house?   1300
But I am thinking not so much of her as for
The children—her the king's friends will make to
    suffer
For what she did. So I have come to save the lives
Of my boys, in case the royal house should harm
    them
While taking vengeance for their mother's wicked
    deed.   1305

Chorus
O Jason, if you but knew how deeply you are
Involved in sorrow, you would not have spoken so.

Jason
What is it? That she is planning to kill me also?

Chorus
Your children are dead, and by their own mother's
  hand.

Jason
What! That is it? O woman, you have destroyed me!   1310

Chorus
You must make up your mind your children are no
  more.

Jason
Where did she kill them? Was it here or in the house?

Chorus
Open the gates and there you will see them murdered.

Jason
Quick as you can unlock the doors, men, and undo
The fastenings and let me see this double evil,   1315
My children dead and her—Oh her I will repay.

> (*His attendants rush to the door. Medea appears
> above the house in a chariot drawn by
> dragons. She has the dead bodies
> of the children with her.*)

Medea
Why do you batter these gates and try to unbar them,
Seeking the corpses and for me who did the deed?
You may cease your trouble, and, if you have need
  of me,
Speak, if you wish. You will never touch me with
  your hand,   1320
Such a chariot has Helius, my father's father,
Given me to defend me from my enemies.

Jason
You hateful thing, you woman most utterly loathed
By the gods and me and by all the race of mankind,
You who have had the heart to raise a sword against   1325

Your children, you, their mother, and left me
    childless—
You have done this, and do you still look at the sun
And at the earth, after these most fearful doings?
I wish you dead. Now I see it plain, though at that
    time
I did not, when I took you from your foreign home   1330
And brought you to a Greek house, you, an evil thing,
A traitress to your father and your native land.
The gods hurled the avenging curse of yours on me.
For your own brother you slew at your own hearthside,
And then came aboard that beautiful ship, the Argo.   1335
And that was your beginning. When you were married
To me, your husband, and had borne children to me,
For the sake of pleasure in the bed you killed them.
There is no Greek woman who would have dared
    such deeds,
Out of all those whom I passed over and chose you   1340
To marry instead, a bitter destructive match,
A monster, not a woman, having a nature
Wilder than that of Scylla in the Tuscan sea.
Ah! no, not if I had ten thousand words of shame
Could I sting you. You are naturally so brazen.   1345
Go, worker in evil, stained with your children's blood.
For me remains to cry aloud upon my fate,
Who will get no pleasure from my newly wedded love,
And the boys whom I begot and brought up, never
Shall I speak to them alive. Oh, my life is over!   1350

Medea

Long would be the answer which I might have
    made to
These words of yours, if Zeus the father did not know
How I have treated you and what you did to me.
No, it was not to be that you should scorn my love,
And pleasantly live your life through, laughing at me;   1355
Nor would the princess, nor he who offered the match,
Creon, drive me away without paying for it.

So now you may call me a monster, if you wish,
A Scylla housed in the caves of the Tuscan sea.
I too, as I had to, have taken hold of your heart. 1360

Jason
You feel the pain yourself. You share in my sorrow.

Medea
Yes, and my grief is gain when you cannot mock it.

Jason
O children, what a wicked mother she was to you!

Medea
They died from a disease they caught from their
    father.

Jason
I tell you it was not my hand that destroyed them. 1365

Medea
But it was your insolence, and your virgin wedding.

Jason
And just for the sake of that you chose to kill them.

Medea
Is love so small a pain, do you think, for a woman?

Jason
For a wise one, certainly. But you are wholly evil.

Medea
The children are dead. I say this to make you suffer. 1370

Jason
The children, I think, will bring down curses on you.

Medea
The gods know who was the author of this sorrow.

Jason
Yes, the gods know indeed, they know your loathsome
    heart.

Medea
Hate me. But I tire of your barking bitterness.

Jason
And I of yours. It is easier to leave you.   1375

Medea
How then? What shall I do? I long to leave you too.

Jason
Give me the bodies to bury and to mourn them.

Medea
No, that I will not. I will bury them myself,
Bearing them to Hera's temple on the promontory;
So that no enemy may evilly treat them   1380
By tearing up their grave. In this land of Corinth
I shall establish a holy feast and sacrifice
Each year forever to atone for the blood guilt.
And I myself go to the land of Erechtheus
To dwell in Aegeus' house, the son of Pandion.   1385
While you, as is right, will die without distinction,
Struck on the head by a piece of the Argo's timber,
And you will have seen the bitter end of my love.

Jason
May a Fury for the children's sake destroy you,
And justice, Requitor of blood.   1390

Medea
What heavenly power lends an ear
To a breaker of oaths, a deceiver?

Jason
Oh, I hate you, murderess of children.

Medea
Go to your palace. Bury your bride.

Jason
I go, with two children to mourn for.   1395

Medea
Not yet do you feel it. Wait for the future.

Jason
Oh, children I loved!

Medea
                    I loved them, you did not.

Jason
You loved them, and killed them.

Medea
                              To make you feel pain.

Jason
Oh, wretch that I am, how I long
To kiss the dear lips of my children!   1400

Medea
Now you would speak to them, now you would kiss
    them.
Then you rejected them.

Jason
                    Let me, I beg you,
Touch my boys' delicate flesh.

Medea
I will not. Your words are all wasted.

Jason
O God, do you hear it, this persecution,   1405
These my sufferings from this hateful
Woman, this monster, murderess of children?
Still what I can do that I will do:
I will lament and cry upon heaven,
Calling the gods to bear me witness   1410
How you have killed my boys and prevent me from
Touching their bodies or giving them burial.
I wish I had never begot them to see them
Afterward slaughtered by you.

Chorus

Zeus in Olympus is the overseer   1415
Of many doings. Many things the gods
Achieve beyond our judgment. What we thought
Is not confirmed and what we thought not God
Contrives. And so it happens in this story.

(*Curtain.*)

THE HERACLEIDAE

(THE CHILDREN OF HERACLES)

Translated by Ralph Gladstone

INTRODUCTION TO
THE HERACLEIDAE

The Legend

EURYSTHEUS, king of Argos, was given control over his cousin Heracles through the contrivance of Hera. He persecuted Heracles throughout that hero's life, sending him on the famous and perilous "Labors." After Heracles had died and been transformed into a god, Eurystheus continued to persecute the family. Wherever these disinherited refugees went, he would send his herald to demand that they be denied sanctuary. He was the most powerful king in Greece, and none dared resist him. But in Attica the Heracleidae finally found a state which was willing to defend their rights; and when Eurystheus invaded Attica to claim them by force, he was defeated and killed.

Such were the main outlines of the legend, at least the Athenian legend (there was a Theban variant as well). Aeschylus had written a tragedy on the subject, and Athenian playwrights loved to glorify an ancient Athens which had stood up for the weak and the oppressed (Aeschylus, *The Eumenides;* Sophocles, *Oedipus at Colonus;* Euripides, *The Suppliant Women, Medea, Heracles*). There are certain details which Euripides either invented or chose to emphasize. He is the first, as far as we know, to bring in the self-immolation of a daughter of Heracles. He also makes a major character out of Iolaus, Heracles' nephew and old companion-in-arms, at the expense of Hyllus, the eldest of the Heracleidae. Some said Hyllus killed Eurystheus, others that Iolaus did. Euripides makes Hyllus a son who is of fighting age, and the messenger's account of the battle gives him an honorable part, but Hyllus never appears on stage. The leader of the Heracleidae is Iolaus, a decrepit but indomitable warrior who is rejuvenated in the course of battle and becomes the hero of the day. Finally, instead of having Eurystheus killed in battle (all other authorities do, as far as we know), Euripides makes Iolaus take him prisoner and have him handed over to Alcmene, who puts him to death over the protests of the Athenians. This last feature may have a bearing on the date and occasion of the play.

The Date

No date for this play has been given by ancient authorities. The versification has technical qualities which find a parallel in three early-dated tragedies: *Alcestis* (438 B.C.), *Medea* (431 B.C.), and *Hippolytus* (428 B.C.). The dating and interpretation may be further helped if we consider an event which took place between autumn of 430 and winter or early spring of 429 B.C. At that time Athens was at war with the Peloponnesian League. Five Peloponnesian envoys, on their way to the king of Persia, were treacherously seized by friends of the Athenians in Thrace, brought to Athens, and there "put to death on the day of their arrival, without trial and without permission to say some things they wished to say" (Thucydides ii. 67.4; also mentioned by Herodotus vii. 137.3). Since our play deals with the summary execution of an unarmed prisoner and was written at some date not far from 430, we can hardly ignore this event. Of course, *The Heracleidae* may have been written and produced earlier; but if we date it just after the execution of the envoys, we may understand why Euripides chose to end the play with the execution of Eurystheus instead of his death in battle.

This abruptly changes the whole direction of the play and reverses our sympathies. From the beginning, we have been made to take the side of the innocent Heracleidae and their gallant protectors against the wicked king, who, not content with his abuse of the father, insists on hunting the children and their feeble guardians to death. It is as simple as that, sheer white against black. The outrageousness of the Argive king is aggravated by a truculent herald; the virtue of the afflicted by the self-sacrifice of a virgin martyr. But when at last Eurystheus appears, he is nothing like his herald; he frankly admits his past misdeeds, neither extenuating nor boasting, and faces death with calm dignity. It is Alcmene who turns horrible in her insistence on revenge, while the Athenians (represented by the chorus) appear, though Euripides does his best for them, as nothing much better than weak well-meaners.

Why has this been done, when following the accepted (so we presume) legend and having Eurystheus killed in battle would have meant an acceptable "straight" play? Euripides knew that brutality brutalizes; people who have been injured or abused too long become worse than their tormentors (Medea, Hecuba, Creusa, Electra, Orestes, Dionysus). But this reversal is uncommonly sudden and lacks the careful and convincing motivation which we find in *Medea, Ion, Orestes,* and elsewhere. I would hazard a guess that the envoys were executed in the winter, not very long before the spring productions; that Euripides was still at work on *The Heracleidae,* and the event made him change the end of the play to suit the occasion. There are certain signs of haste in the writing. Euripides obviously could and did write iambics at breakneck speed, but *The Heracleidae* has a smaller proportion of the far more difficult choral lyric than any other Euripidean play. If the manuscript is sound (but it may not be) the end of the play is carelessly composed. One other point is the more than usual emphasis on woman's place in a modest, but determined, maiden's apology for public appearance; it recalls the pronouncement of Pericles in the winter of 431–430 to the effect that women should not even be seen, much less heard (Thucydides ii. 45.2).

My guess, then, is spring 429 B.C. for this play. The execution was a horror, the worse because just retaliation was pleaded, as if two wrongs were to make a right. But both Athens and Sparta were to do far worse still. This play has an Athens still unbrutalized, though acquiescent; it is the wronged and rescued suppliants who turn beastly; and who are these but the ancestors of the Lacedaemonians, after all? The Argives (neutral in 429; but one Argive *was* executed at Athens) are not so bad as we thought, though all heralds grow arrogant on their sacred immunity. There is plenty of "glorious Athens," and "liberty" is a key word. But Athens has slipped, this once. Euripides' faith in his city is not to be broken for a long time, but here is reproof and warning.

The Play

It is rapid, with little lyric or high poetry, not profound but, despite the melodrama, often shrewd. The young king is really a democrat in disguise; will do nothing without the people's consent; and therefore, while ready to protect the afflicted, cannot help wishing (like the king in *The Suppliants* of Aeschylus) that these particular suppliants had never come his way. Macaria seems a mere abstraction of virtue, until her outburst at Iolaus, when he offers to spoil her act, shows her as human after all. The most challenging piece of treatment is that accorded to Iolaus. Why must he be so old? We are not to press legendary ages, but, after all, Iolaus was of the generation of Hyllus, not of Alcmene; he was the nephew of Heracles, not his uncle. Probably, for one thing, for the story. The point is that the Heracleidae are helpless until helped by Athens and cannot be protected by two strong fighters of their own. So Hyllus comes in as an afterthought and is kept (with his army) off stage, while Iolaus is superannuated. Therefore, also, Demophon is king of Athens instead of Good King Theseus, as in other versions; Demophon can be more plausibly represented as a younger man. But also the theme of resolute old age and of rejuvenation seems to fascinate the tragedian. The prototype is Laertes in the 24th book of the *Odyssey*. But it has been suggested that Aeschylus in his lost play rejuvenated Iolaus, and, if so, Euripides is (as elsewhere) having his fun with

Aeschylus. For there is irony, at least, in the treatment of Iolaus. As to whether the miracle ever took place at all, the messenger prefaces his account in the best manner of Herodotus, the scientific historian of the day: "Up to this point [the prayer of Iolaus] I am telling you what I saw; for what followed, I am telling you what they tell me." Note that no rejuvenated Iolaus returns to the stage. The going forth to battle of Iolaus is indisputably comic, though it is that tragic funniness that makes old age so cruel (Aeschylus with Cilissa in *The Libation Bearers,* the Prophetess in *The Eumenides*). As so often, Euripides has tried to cram too much into one play, to move in too many directions at once; but he has made livelier what started as a most conventional piece.

One feature of the play is the supernumerary male children of Heracles. They are on stage, presumably, from start to finish, though they say nothing. The play is named from them, not, as usually, from the chorus or a principal character. Neither the daughter of Heracles nor the herald is named in the text. The names Macaria and Copreus are in the ancient *dramatis personae.* The latter comes from the *Iliad.* The scene is at Marathon, on the coast of Attica.

CHARACTERS

Iolaus, an old man and friend of Heracles

Copreus, herald of Eurystheus

Chorus of old men of Marathon

Demophon, son of Theseus and king of Athens

Macaria, daughter of Heracles

Alcmene, mother of Heracles

Attendants

Eurystheus, king of Argos and Mycenae

Small children of Heracles, guards, townspeople

THE HERACLEIDAE

SCENE: *Before the Temple of Zeus at Marathon.*
(Iolaus, accompanied by small children
of Heracles, enters.)

Iolaus
For years I've known that anyone who's just
Is born to serve his neighbors, but the man
Who will persist in feathering his nest
Has got no public spirit and is hard
To deal with, as I've found out to my cost.   5
And though I could have lived respectably
In Argos, with my family and in peace,
As right-hand man of Heracles, I served
Through his worst trials, while he still was alive.
Now he's in heaven, and as guardian of   10
His children, I could use a guard myself.
When he was dead and gone, Eurystheus
Decided to eliminate us, too.
We got away, and, though we saved our skins,
Our home is gone; and now we stand condemned   15
To keep on wandering from state to state,
Because this king, whose record is as black
As sin, has had the front to lay on us
A new humiliation. Anywhere
We go, when he finds out, he sends someone   20
To bully them into expelling us,
And claims his town's too strong and he's too rich
To risk offending. When our hosts recall
That *these* are orphans, that *I've* no support,
They cringe and end by sending us away.   25
With displaced children I displace myself

To share with those who have more than their share
Of sorrows. If I left them, men might say,
"He failed to do his duty by them, once
Their father died, in spite of family ties."   30
And since the rest of Greece is banned to us,
We've reached the neighborhood of Marathon
To throw ourselves upon the mercy of
The gods and seek their help. Two kings, I'm told,
Of Pandion's and Theseus' line have here   35
Come into power, both our relatives.
That's why we've come to the world-famous state
Of Athens, on a trip conceived and planned
By two old strategists. So I, for one,
Am seeing to the safety of these boys.   40
Meanwhile Alcmene minds the girls and keeps
Them all inside the temple. It would look
Highly improper if we let them stand
In front of it, exposed to people's eyes.
Then Hyllus and the older boys have gone   45
To find another refuge, jus in case
We ever should be forced to leave this town.
Quick, children! Come back! Hold on tight!
That's Eurystheus' herald coming here,
The one that has us chased from place to place,   50

(*Enter Copreus.*)

And made us homeless refugees. Scum!
I'll see you damned and your employer too.
Why, you're the selfsame man who used to bring
Bad news repeatedly to Heracles.

Copreus
Oh come now, do you really think you've found   55
A refuge and protection? Are you mad
Enough to think that anyone would choose
Your helplessness in preference to our strength?
Why don't you stop this fuss? You're bound to come
Right back to Argos and a stony end.   60

128

Iolaus

Not on your life! I'm well protected by
God's temple and this free and sovereign state.

Copreus

Oh, then you'll give my muscles exercise?

Iolaus

You wouldn't dare to take us out by force.

Copreus

You'll soon see how wrong that prediction is.   65

(Tries to seize children.)

Iolaus

Then over my dead body, if you do.

Copreus

Keep out of this. I need no leave from you
To take away my master's property.

(Throws Iolaus down.)

Iolaus

Help! Men of this historic town, though we're
Protected by Zeus's temple in the square,   70
We've been assaulted and our wreaths defiled,
Which outrages the city and the gods!

Chorus

You there! Just what's the meaning of all this
Ungodly noise, and by the altar too?
Oh! This poor old man is lying   75
On the ground. What a shameful thing!
Who was it handled you so brutally?   .

Iolaus

This man here dragged me from the altar by
Main force, and showed contempt for all your gods.

Chorus

What country are you coming from, old man?   80

Have you reached these federated states
By the blade of the oar in the sea? Were you
Rowed over here from some Euboean port?

Iolaus
No, we're no islanders. We've made our way
To Athens from Mycenae.   85

Chorus
And what name did you go by
Among the Mycenaean citizens?

Iolaus
You've heard of me, I think. I'm Iolaus,
Known as the right-hand man of Heracles.

Chorus
The name has a familiar ring. But please,   90
Why don't you tell us whose young children these
Are, whom you're leading by the hand?

Iolaus
These are the sons of Heracles, who've come
To ask protection here from you and yours.

Chorus
Just what is it you want of us? Are you   95
Applying for a hearing here?

Iolaus
We ask you to stand by us and to keep
The Argives from abducting us by force.

Copreus
That's hardly good enough. Your betters here
Have found you and will have the final say.   100

Chorus
The rights of those the gods protect
Are bound to be respected. To go off
And leave an altar desecrated makes
A mockery of justice.

Copreus
Who spoke of such a thing? I'm asking you   105
To drive my master's subjects from the land.

Chorus
That would be sacrilegious,
Rejecting people who demand our help.

Copreus
It would be healthier to change your minds
And keep your city out of trouble's way.   110

Chorus
Instead of kidnapping these refugees
So brazenly, you should have seen the king
And shown respect for Athens' sovereign rights.

Copreus
Now that you mention it, who is the king?

Chorus
Demophon, son of the great Theseus.   115

Copreus
Oh, then my business lies with him! All this
Is just a waste of breath and nothing more.

Chorus
Look! There he comes, and his brother Acamas.
They're hurrying to judge this whole affair.

(*Enter Demophon, with Acamas.*)

Demophon
Since you old men rushed here upon the scene,   120
Before the young ones helped or reached the shrine,
Suppose you tell us just what's drawn this crowd?

Chorus
These children, who have hung the altar with
The wreaths you see, are Heracles' sons.
Iolaus was their father's right-hand man.   125

131

Demophon
But why were there such awful cries for help?

Chorus
That man just tried to drag them all away,
Which caused the cries we heard. The way he threw
That poor old man down touched me to the heart.

Demophon
Although he looks and dresses like a Greek,   130
It needs a savage to behave like that.
Stranger, it's up to you. Be quick and let
Me know what sort of country you come from.

Copreus
Well, since you ask, I come from Argos. Now
I'll tell who sent me and just why I'm here.   135
It was Eurystheus of Mycenae told
Me to come here and bring these back. I have
Authority for all I do or say;
Since, as an Argive, I'm recovering
These Argive nationals who've run away,   140
Though legally condemned to death at home.
We have a perfect right to carry out
The laws we make for our own sovereign land.
I've often made this point, each time I reached
A new "protector." Not a single one   145
Was ever rash enough to play with fire.
Now they've come here. Why, they must take you for
Colossal fools, or else they want to take
One reckless chance and get it over with.
They can't think seriously that you alone   150
Of all the Greeks they've seen would feel for them
In their sad state, unless you'd lost your minds;
Consider what you stand to gain if you
Should let them in or let us take them out.
For our part we can offer to you all   155
The weight of power; our king's great influence
Will be behind your town in all you do.

But if their artful talk and wailing move
Your pity, that can only mean one thing.
A total war! Don't you believe that we'll   160
Give up our fight and bring no steel into play.
But why should you provoke us? Have we seized
What's yours? Are we aggressors? Or is your
Allies' security at stake? What kind
Of cause is this to die for? Your own men   165
Will surely curse your name if you insist
On scuttling everything so recklessly
For these young brats and this half-dead old man.
You may believe the long view bears you out,
But that will hardly help you now, my friend.   170
These boys would never stand against our arms,
Not even as grown men, as you may hope.
Well, anyhow that day's far off, and you'll
Be dealt with in the meantime; take my word
For that. We're asking nothing, but we want   175
To take back what is ours. I know that you
Are in the habit of declaring for
The underdog by choice. I warn you. Don't.

Chorus
It's very hard to judge or understand
A case like this until we've heard both sides.   180

Iolaus
I'll say in your land's favor, Majesty,
I'm not being driven out of *here* at least
Until I've listened and have had my say.
This man is nothing to us, and we want
No part of Argos. That's been so since they   185
Passed sentence on us; we're expatriates.
What earthly right has he to drag us all
Back to the town that drove us out, as though
They still had claims on us? We're aliens now.
Must Argive exiles leave the rest of Greece?   190
You can't intimidate Athenians
And make them drive out Heracles' own sons.

This isn't an Achaean town, you know,
Or Trachis, so your heavy-handed ways
Of getting temples to evict us and   195
Your saber-rattling will not work here.
If I were wrong, and you should have your way,
This wouldn't be the free state that I know.
But I *do* know what stuff they're made of here.
They'd sooner die. Like all right-thinking men   200
They're sure that death is better than disgrace.
So much for Athens. It's a bad mistake
To overpraise, and I myself have been
Annoyed at getting more than was my due.
But, I'll explain why you're in duty bound   205
To save these boys, as ruler of this land.
Pittheus was Pelops' son and in his turn
Sired Aethra, who gave birth to Theseus,
Your father. Now, to come back to these boys,
Their father springs from Zeus and Alcmene,   210
And she was Pelops' daughter, which would make
Near cousins of your father and of theirs.
So much for ties of blood, and now I'll tell
What else obliges you to stand up for them.
I carried Heracles' own shield upon   215
The bloody expedition to bring back
For Theseus the Amazon queen's belt.
And Heracles, as every Greek knows, saved
Your father from the moated depths of hell.
And in return, what they now ask of you   220
Is not to be betrayed, not to be torn
By force from altars and from your frontiers.
It would be a disgrace for you, for all
Of Athens to let refugees—and those
Your cousins, too—be dragged off. Oh, my God!   225
Just look at them! On my knees I beg of you!
For pity's sake! Oh please don't let them go!
The sons of Heracles are in your hands.
Then prove yourself their cousin and their friend,

Their father, brother, ruler, all in one,   230
Rather than throw them to their enemies.

Chorus
This story touches all our hearts. We've seen
Now for the first time what it is to be
Well-born, yet in distress. Nobility
Can suffer, and through no fault of its own.   235

Demophon
Three factors have decided me against
Expelling, Iolaus, friends and guests.
For, first and foremost, you took refuge at
God's altar, with these children at your side.
Then family ties, and for our father's sake,   240
A debt of honor to be kind to them.
Last, but not least, concern for my prestige.
If I let strangers break the temple bounds,
Then everyone will say we gave these up
To Argos out of fear and that we're not   245
Our own real masters here. I'd sooner die.
Don't be afraid. I wish you could have come
In better days, but nobody would dare
To touch you or the children while you're here.

                                            (*To Herald.*)

Go back home, and there say to your king   250
He'll have a hearing if he likes, but you
Won't take these refugees away with you.

Copreus
Not even if my claim is right and wins?

Demophon
What? Right to drag off refugees by force?

Copreus
If I get a bad name, it won't hurt you.   255

Demophon
But I will too, if I let you drag them home.

Copreus
Just banish them, I'll do the rest myself.

Demophon
You fool! To think you can outwit the god!

Copreus
This is a nest for outlaws, I can see.

Demophon
The temple gives protection to all men.   260

Copreus
My countrymen may not agree with you.

Demophon
But I'm the master when in my own house.

Copreus
If you behave yourself and don't harm us.

Demophon
I'll chance that rather than outrage the gods.

Copreus
I wouldn't want to see you fighting us.   265

Demophon
No more would I, but still I'll stand by these.

Copreus
I'll take what's mine back with me, just the same.

Demophon
You think so? Well, you won't get very far.

Copreus
In any case I'll try the thing and see.

                    (*Tries to seize children again.*)

Demophon
You'll lay a hand on them at your own risk!   270

                    (*Makes threatening motion.*)

Chorus
For heaven's sake, don't hit a diplomat.

Demophon
Then let the diplomat behave himself.

Chorus
Yes, go away. Don't touch him, Majesty!

Copreus
I'm going, since I'm quite outnumbered here.
But I'll return with armies at my back.   275
There's an enormous army waiting for
Me with Eurystheus at the head. He's at
The boundaries of Alcathus' own state
And stands on the alert. So when he hears
Of this disgrace, he'll strike you like a flash,   280
You and your land and every living thing.
What are our soldiers for if not to fight
And punish you, who give us ample cause?

Demophon
To hell with you! Your Argos won't make me
Give in an inch, and you won't drag these off   285
And shame us, since we take no orders here
From Argos, but we do just as we like.

(*Exit Copreus.*)

Chorus
Time to think about defense
Before their army strikes our soil.
Argives were always bloodthirsty, but now   290
What they'll soon learn will make them twice as
    fierce.
Since diplomats are all alike and will
Distort and magnify what they've gone through.
I know he'll tell his lord he was so
Mistreated here that, all in all,   295
He barely got his skin away.

Iolaus
There's nothing better for a boy than to
Have had a good and noble father and
To marry well. I can't approve of those
Who go below their station out of love   300
And compromise their sons through their own lust.
Since noble people stand adversity
Much better than the mob; for instance, we
Were at our last gasp, till we found these friends
And relatives. Alone of all the Greeks,   305
They've dared to stand up and defend our rights.
There, children, go and give your hand to them,
And you give your hand too. Now, go ahead!
O children, these are really friends in need.
If you should ever see your native land   310
And home again and there receive your due,
Remember them as friends who saved your lives.
With this in mind, don't ever fight with them
At all, but treat them as your best allies.
They've earned your full respect by taking on   315
A formidable enemy on our
Account. Though we'd no place to lay our heads,
They didn't drive us out or let us go
For all of that. And I for one must say
That while I live and breathe—and after, too—   320
I'll honor you like Theseus and I'll sing
Your praises everywhere and tell the world
How well you treated and protected these
Young children. You've kept up your father's name
In Greece. You're living up to the high standard   325
Set by your great family in every way.
That's most unusual. You'll find, I think,
That very few men match their fathers now.

Chorus
We've always felt it was the decent thing
To succor men who couldn't help themselves.   330

We've fought for others many times before,
And now we see a new war coming up.

Demophon
Thank you. I'm sure of your sincerity,
Old man, and that you're grateful, as you say.
And now I've got to mobilize my men   335
And station them so that the enemy
Will get a hot reception. First my scouts
Will go to see we're not caught by surprise.
The Argives waste no time in their attacks.
Meanwhile I'll sacrifice with seers, but   340
You take the children from this altar and
Go to my palace. You'll be in good hands
While this keeps me away. Why, go ahead.

Iolaus
No, I'll stay at the altar. We'll sit down
And wait and pray until you've won the fight.   345
And when your triumph is complete, we'll go
Home with you. I think that the gods
On our side are more than a match for theirs.
Hera may be their patron but we have
Athena; and what counts in the long run   350
Is having stronger gods upon your side.
Pallas will never let the others win.

(*Exit Demophon.*)

Chorus

STROPHE

Then brag away until you're hoarse.
But know that Argive bluster can't
Affect our minds, nor can it force   355
Us to turn tail. Not for such rant
As this of yours to bring our great
And lovely city down so low
And leave her prey to such a fate.
To think you and your king are so   360
Crack-brained as that!

EURIPIDES

ANTISTROPHE

To kidnap refugees, and those
The wards of both our gods and men,
Is bad enough, for one who knows
Our state's as good as yours; and then   365
To have a stranger treat our king
Like dirt, without a single claim
To right and justice is a thing
That only fools and men past shame
Can well defend.   370

EPODE

We're peaceful men, but in advance
We warn a king who's gone berserk
To keep away. He'll have no chance
To carry out his dirty work.
Though butchery's his special field,   375
We'll hold our own if it should come
To handling a spear or shield.
He'd better keep his creatures from
Attacking Athens, hold his hand,
And not pollute our lovely land.   380

(Re-enter Demophon.)

Iolaus

My son, why are you looking so depressed?
Bad news about the Argive movements? Don't
Keep us all guessing. Is all quiet or
Are they advancing? What their herald said
Is worth attention, as their king will come   385
Here as the pet of chance and of the gods,
And cordially detests this city, to boot.
Still, in the end, Zeus sees to it that no
One can afford such high and mighty airs.

Demophon

The Argives and their king are on the way.
I've reconnoitered, since a man who sets   390

Up for a decent general has got
To see these things himself, not second-hand.
They haven't reached the plain; their leader keeps
Them on the rocky cliff. He's looking for
A way to bring his army to the heart   395
Of Attica, and camp there, I should think,
Without unnecessary risk. And our
Own preparations are complete; the town
Is on a battle footing. We're about
To offer all the things up to the gods   400
Required to save us and to win the fight.
While priests are sacrificing everywhere,
I've had all oracles, all old and well-known
Or confidential forecasts analyzed
To find out what to do. In most respects   405
They varied a great deal, but in one thing
They tally every one: we have to give
Up to Demeter's child as victim a
Young lady of respectable descent.
Now you'll admit, I've done my best for you.   410
But I can hardly kill my child, or force
Another citizen to such a point.
Only a lunatic would let his child
Be killed that way, and angry groups in all
The streets are thrashing out the question now.   415
Some say we're bound to fight for refugees;
While others claim I've acted like a fool.
So if I did this for you, I would have
A full-scale civil war upon my hands.
However, maybe you can find a way   420
To save yourselves and us as well without
My losing face upon this issue. As
I'm not a tyrant over savages,
Good government must be both give and take.

Chorus
We're anxious to defend you, but the gods   425
Now seem determined not to let us fight.

Iolaus

O children, we're like sailors who've set through
A hurricane and almost reached the shore,
Only to have the wind veer round and blow
Us back to sea. And we ourselves are forced   430
Out of the harbor in that same way, although
We'd thought that we were safe inside the port.
O God! How terrible to have a hope
That charms and cheats you. Still, I know that you
Are not to blame. I can't expect you to   435
Kill off your subjects' children. This whole state
Has done its best. Although the gods see fit
To treat us this way, still I won't forget.
I don't know what to do, boys, since we've no
More refuges to try, and no more gods   440
To pray to, no more countries in the world
To emigrate to. We're as good as gone.
The game is up. I don't care for myself,
Although I hate to let the Argives have
The joy of killing me; it's you that drive   445
Me frantic, and your poor old grandmother,
Brought down so low at such a time of life!
But all I've gone through doesn't count at all;
We're absolutely destined from the start
To fall and be cut down like animals.   450
Yet maybe you can think of something. I
Still think there may be some way out; why don't
You give me up instead of these young boys
And save their lives without risk to yourself?
That's it! I've got no cause to hang onto   455
My life, and their king would be very pleased
To catch and torture Heracles' good friend.
The man's quite low enough. A man with brains
Had better fight with someone of his class,
And so get decent treatment when he's down.   460

Chorus

Oh please don't put the blame on us. To hear

Ourselves accused of giving you away
Sounds ugly, even though it's not deserved.

Demophon
Said like a gentleman, but it won't do.

(*To Iolaus. Macaria enters while he speaks.*)

The king's not marching here for you; an old   465
Man's not worth bothering about. It's these
He wants to put out of the way, since, as
He's very well aware, young nobles with
A family score to settle can, when they
Grow up, make matters awkward for him then.   470
If you've another plan, let's hear it, since,
I don't mind telling you, these oracles
Have got me worried and at my wit's end.

Macaria
Strangers, before all else, I hope you won't
Think it was brazen of me to come out.   475
I know a woman should be quiet and
Discreet, and that her place is in the home.
Yet I came out because I heard your cries. (*Speaking
     to Iolaus.*)
Although I'm not the family head, I have
A right to be concerned about the fate   480
Of my own brothers, and I'd like to know,
For my sake too, what new thing has turned up
To plague you—as if this were not enough.

Iolaus
I've always thought your family contains
No cooler head than yours, Macaria.   485
The fact is, just when things were going well,
We suddenly fell downward with a crash,
Back where we were. The king's priests say he has
To sacrifice—not just a bull or calf—
A real live girl, of noble stock, to please   490
Persephone, if any of us here

Values his life. And that's our quandary.
The king won't kill a stranger's child, much less
His own, and hinted pretty plainly that
If we see no way out, we'll have to find   495
Another refuge. As for him, he's bound
To think of his own country's safety first.

Macaria
And on that issue, then, we stand or fall?

Iolaus
All other matters being equal, yes.

Macaria
Then all your Argive fears are over, since   500
This volunteer is quite prepared to die,
And let herself be led off to the slaughter.
What could we say if Athens were to court
This frightful danger just for us, and we
Left all the brunt to them, and wouldn't help   505
Ourselves because we couldn't bear the thought
Of death. To keep on sniveling like this
At altars while we show to all the world
Our cowardice would admirably fit
Our father's name, or is it like the brave   510
To make fools of themselves? I'd sooner see
This city taken—God forbid—and let
Myself be caught and have worst come to worst
To Heracles' own child, and die that way.
If I give in and leave here, then how shall   515
I look when people ask why trembling slaves
Like us have come to ask protection there.
They'll turn us out and say they're not disposed
To lift a finger for such spineless things.
Why, even if I did survive the deaths   520
Of my own brothers, I'd have no hope left
(Though people have been known to sell their friends
Upon that chance). But who would marry me,
Or want this friendless girl as mother of

His sons? To end things now is much to be   525
Preferred to *that* shame, even though a girl
Not so well-known might well make the other choice.
Come, lead me to the place where I'm to die.
Then wreathe me and begin whenever you like;
And go and win the fight. I hereby put   530
Myself on record that of my free will
I volunteer to die for these and for
Myself. The brave have found no finer prize
Than leaving life the way it should be done.

Chorus

A girl who gives her own life to save these   535
And says such things leaves nothing unsaid.
No words could be compared to hers; no acts
Of flesh and blood rank higher than her own.

Iolaus

There speaks the hero's daughter, Heracles'
Own child. At any rate, there's no way to   540
Mistake *your* family tree. But, though I'm proud
Of what you've said, your plight goes to my heart.
Yet there's a better way. You ought to call
Your sisters and draw lots to choose the one
Who'll die to save us all. Why, otherwise,   545
It isn't fair for you to die this way.

Macaria

I *won't* be butchered as a gambling debt.
No, it won't do; there's nothing fine in that.
But if you'll take me and consent to use
Me of yourselves, I offer up my life   550
For them of my own accord, but won't be forced.

Iolaus

Wonder of wonders!
That answer was more splendid than the fine
One that you made before, if anything;
And you outdo yourself in pluck and sense.   555

145

I can't tell you to die or not to die,
Although your death will save your brothers' lives.

Macaria
Well put. Don't worry, no guilt can attach
To you, since I myself elect to die.
Come on; I'd like to have you hold me when   560
I die, and cover me up afterward,
Since now it's time to go to meet the knife,
If I'm my father's daughter, as I claim.

Iolaus
Oh, no, I couldn't bear to watch you die.

Macaria
Then ask the king to let me end my days   565
In women's hands, and not the hands of men.

Demophon
Poor girl! Of course, I never could forgive
Myself if I forgot the honors due
You, and God knows I've cause enough not to:
Your grit, your honest heart, such courage as   570
I've never known a woman show before.
Well, go ahead and speak to the old man
And children here, if you've a last request.

Macaria
This is goodbye. Please bring my brothers up
To be as wise as you, no more, no less,   575
In all, and I'll be satisfied. I count
On you to do your loyal best to save
Them, since we're your brood in a way, and raised
By your hands, and I'm giving up my prime
And chance for marriage just to die for them.   580
And now I wish to all my brothers here
The best of everything, and may you win
The things for which I'm staking my own life.
Be sure to pay respect to this old man
And your old grandmother inside as well,   585

And these good people. If the gods will let
You find relief and see your home again,
Remember to give the girl that saved your lives
The kind of funeral that she deserves,
Since she played fair with you and gave hers up.   590
These values will sustain me afterward
As spinster, childless. . . . Afterward: is there
An afterward? I hope not. If there's *then*
No end to all our troubles, where do we
Go on from there—since death itself, they say,   595
Supplies the cure for everything that ails?

Iolaus

As bravest of your sex, be sure that we
Would never think of failing to pay you
The highest honors, here and when you're gone.
And so Godspeed, saving the pardon of   600
The goddess in whose hands your life is placed.

                              (*Exit Macaria.*)

This shock's too much for me, and everything

                              (*Totters.*)

Is going black. Quick, children, prop me up!
Let me sit down and cover me with these.
To flout the oracle would be the end of all   605
Of us; though this alternative is sad,
Still, it's the lesser evil of the two.

Chorus

STROPHE

In all our ups and downs a wise
Man knows the gods have final say,
Nor can one house monopolize   610
Destiny, but from day to day
Luck pirouettes, and people who
Had conquered stoop, while drudges make
Their fortunes overnight. But you
Cannot get out of it or break   615

Through by chicanery. You'll find
To try's a waste, time out of mind.

ANTISTROPHE

Don't take God's orders lying down
Or fret because Macaria's won   620
A high and durable renown
For kin and country. She's undone,
For doing what will send her through
The ages. A stout heart commands
Its way through pain. In that she's true   625
To everything her father stands
For and her birthright, true as steel.
The brave are gone; the quick must feel.

(Enter Attendant.)

Attendant
Come, children, can you tell where Iolaus   630
And your own grandmother have gone from here?

Iolaus
Why here I am, as far as that's concerned.

Attendant
Reclining, with your head bowed down! What for?

Iolaus
The troubles of those near to me strike home.

Attendant
Well, now you can get up. Look at me, man.   635

Iolaus
I'm old and these old bones have got no strength.

Attendant
But I have news for you, and what news too!

Iolaus
Who are you? Where have I seen you before?

148

Attendant
I'm Hyllus' servant. Don't you know me yet?

Iolaus
You're a real friend! You're here to save us all?   640

Attendant
Yes, everything is going to be all right.

Iolaus
Alcmene, come on out. It's you I want
To hear the wonderful news this man's brought.
You've worried yourself sick for so long now
About your grandsons' trip. They're back at last.   645

(*Enter Alcmene.*)

Alcmene
What's wrong? What's causing all this noise that fills
The house? Another Argive to assault
You? Stranger, I warn you. I'm weak, God knows
But I'll fight kidnappers till my last breath,
Or Heracles was not his mother's son.   650
If you so much as lay a hand upon
These children, then you'll have the glory of
Attacking two defenseless oldsters first.

Iolaus
Cheer up. There's nothing of the sort. This man
Is not an Argive come to threaten us.   655

Alcmene
Then why cry out and give the sign of fright?

Iolaus
I only cried out to bring you out here.

Alcmene
That's quite another thing. Who is this man?

Iolaus
He's come to tell you that your grandson's here.

Alcmene
Your glad news makes you welcome, as he is.   660
But if he *has* arrived, where is he now?
What kept him from accompanying you
And gladdening his old grandmother's heart?

Attendant
He's halted, and is drawing up his troops.

Alcmene
Well that, of course, is no concern of mine.   665

Iolaus
It is, though I'm the one to ask details.

Attendant
Well, just what is it that you want to know?

Iolaus
How many men did Hyllus bring with him?

Attendant
Plenty. I couldn't tell you more than that.

Iolaus
And Athens' leaders have been notified?   670

Attendant
Yes, and he's stationed to the left of them.

Iolaus
Why they must be about to start the fight?

Attendant
Yes, victims have been brought forth to be killed.

Iolaus
How far from your lines are the enemy?

Attendant
I saw the Argive king plain as could be.   675

Iolaus
Yes? What's he up to? Drawing up his men?

Attendant
Yes, I should think so, though I heard no news.
I'm off to my own chiefs; when action starts
I don't intend to leave them in the lurch.

Iolaus
Well, wait for me! That's just the thing! I want   680
To go and join my friends and help them out.

Attendant
Come now, don't talk such rot. It's not like you.

Iolaus
Not like me, is it, to fight for my friends?

Attendant
You'd do no good, unless your looks could kill.

Iolaus
What? I could smash a shield in just like that!   685

Attendant
You might, if you could keep from falling first.

Iolaus
There's not a one that will stand up to me.

Attendant
There, easy now; you're not the man you were.

Iolaus
I'll take on just as many as I did.

Attendant
Your help won't turn the tide in any case.   690

Iolaus
Don't keep me from a thing I'm set to do.

Attendant
To do? You mean to want it done, don't you?

Iolaus
Say what you please, but still I go along.

Attendant
But you're unarmed. How can you face a fight?

Iolaus
I'll use the captured arms which happen to   695
Be hanging in the temple here. The god
Will get them back if I survive; if not,
He'll never dun me. Go and take them down.
Quick! Bring the gear out here! A stay-at-home
Is a disgrace, that's what he is. He keeps   700
Out of harm's way and shakes, while others fight.

(*Exit Attendant.*)

Chorus
The years have left your spirit just
As fiery, in your faded body.
But why must you try so hard to hurt yourself?
It does *our* state no good, if you can't bring   705
Yourself to act your age and not go off
On useless tangents. No one
Can bring you back your prime again.

Alcmene
What lunacy is this? Do you propose
To leave me and the children here alone?   710

Iolaus
War is a man's job. Your work's minding these.

Alcmene
What's to become of me if you should die?

Iolaus
The grandsons who are left will tend you then.

Alcmene
Suppose worse comes to worst—my God!—for them?

Iolaus
These others will stand by you, never fear.   715

Alcmene
Then here I put my trust, my last resort.

152

Iolaus
I'm sure that Zeus is also on your side.

Alcmene
Hm!
It's not for me to criticize Zeus, but
Still he knows best if he's played fair with me.　　　**720**

(*Re-enter Attendant.*)

Attendant
Here is a full and fitting battle outfit;
Be quick and put it on. The fight's at hand.
For above everything the God of Battles
Detests a slacker. If the gear's too heavy,
Go on without it. Once inside the ranks　　　**725**
You can encase yourself; till then I'll carry it.

Iolaus
All right, come on; but keep my things all ready.
Now put the spear-shaft into my left hand
And take my right arm so, to guide my steps.

Attendant
Ye gods! Am I to nursemaid you to war?　　　**730**

Iolaus
No, but we'll watch our step. To fall's bad luck.

Attendant
If only you could do what you can dream.

Iolaus
Hurry! I can't afford to miss the fight.

Attendant
You are the dawdler, though you think it's I.

Iolaus
But don't you see how very fast I'm walking?　　　**735**

Attendant
I see the speed is largely in your mind.

Iolaus
You'll change your tune as soon as I get there.

Attendant
What will you do? I want to see you win.

Iolaus
You'll see me smash clean through somebody's shield.

Attendant
If ever we arrive there, which I doubt.　　　　　740

Iolaus
I wish, oh arm of mine, that you could help
Me as you used to, when with Heracles
I ravaged Sparta, in my youth and power.
Then how we'd thrash this king, Eurystheus, now,
Who hasn't got the pluck to face a fight.　　　　745
But fortune always will confer an aura
Of worth, unworthily; and in this world
The lucky person passes for a genius.

　　　　　　　　　　　　　　　　(*Exeunt.*)

Chorus
STROPHE
We call earth and the all-night span
Owned by the moon, and on the sun,
The god that radiates to man,　　　　　　　750
To send the word down here. With one
Voice make the whole sky ring like mad
To Zeus's own throne, and all the way
Out to Athena with the glad
News. As for us, we say:　　　　　　　　755
For Athens, home, and for the right
Of refugees, we mean to fight
With naked steel.
ANTISTROPHE
A dreadful and appalling thing
It is, to think that such a great　　　　　760
Town like Mycenae, threatening,

154

Should store up spite against our state.
But we'd have thoroughly deserved
Our ample fill of shame and curses
If, with guest-rights unobserved,   765
We gave to Argos' tender mercies
Their fugitives. Our champion Zeus
Prizes us, nor will I reduce
The gods beneath ourselves.

STROPHE

Mother of our state and Queen!   770
Defender and Mistress as well!
Smash the false attackers' spleen.
Send their serried spears to hell!
Our cause is good, and I refuse
To think that we deserve to lose   775
Our native city.

ANTISTROPHE

We honor the abundant rite
Of yours, and when the month is done,
In sequent song the young and light
Of foot can dance and chant, as one   780
While night brings to the windy hill
The pulse of dance, and girls that fill
The dark with reveling.

(Enter another Attendant.)

Attendant
Madam, the news I bring is short and sweet,
Short in the telling, and yet sweet to hear.   785
We've won and set up a memorial
Hung with a full display of captured arms.

Alcmene
How wonderful! This lucky day has set
You free for all time, since you bring such news.
Yet I'm not free myself of one nightmare: 790
Are all my near and dear ones still alive?

155

Attendant
Alive and well and heroes every one.

Alcmene
And is old Iolaus all right, too?

Attendant
Covered with glory, too, with heaven's help.

Alcmene
What? Has he something to his credit too?   795

Attendant
He's been changed back to a young man again.

Alcmene
Well, of all things! But, first of all, please tell
Us how our soldiers won this victory.

Attendant
I'll give you the whole story here and now.
When we had drawn our own troops up and stood   800
Directly opposite the enemy,
Hyllus dismounted from his chariot.
Standing in no-man's land between the two,
He called to Eurystheus, "What's the use
Of hurting Athens, king? Why not expose   805
Just one man's life, instead of harming your
Land too? I challenge you to fight it out
With me alone. If you win, you can take
The sons of Heracles, and if I do
I'll win my family seat and honor back."   810
And all the army madly cheered the thought
Of Hyllus' pluck and of their own relief.
But not the audience nor sheer concern
For his prestige as leader proved enough
To shame the king there into showing fight.   815
He didn't dare. And that's the kind of man
Who wants to capture Heracles' own sons.
Then Hyllus took his place back in the ranks.
And when the seers realized that there was

No hope of ending matters with a duel,   820
They sacrificed at once, and let the blood
Flow down the victims' throats, in augury.
The chiefs got in their chariots; the rest
Hid ribs with shield-ribs; Demophon cheered on
His troops in language worthy of his birth.   825
"Athenians, this earth that bore and raised
You all, needs you to fight for her today."
Meantime, the other king implored his men
Not to shame Argos' or Mycenae's name,
Until the trumpet call came high and clear.   830
And then both sides closed in. The sound of all
Those shields colliding came in one great crash,
And shrieks and pandemonium broke loose.
At first their spearmen proved too much for us
And drove us back; then they gave ground again,   835
And it was touch and go. We buckled down
To fighting at close quarters, hand to hand.
Men dropped all round as war-cries swept the field.
"Athens, come on." Then "Men of Argos, strike;
Don't let the enemy make fools of us."   840
And we had all that we could do, but with
Great trouble, in the end we broke their ranks.
Then Iolaus, seeing Hyllus rush
By him begged hard to be allowed to get
Up on a chariot. Once there, he took   845
The reins himself and set his course straight for
The Argive king That much I saw myself.
I'll tell the rest as it was told to me.
Passing Pallene and Athena's hill
He saw Eurystheus' car, and so he prayed   850
To Zeus and Hebe, to get back his youth
For just a day, and take a full revenge.
Then came the most astounding thing of all!
Two stars shone on the yoke. They threw a dark
Cloud over the whole car, and people who   855
Should know say they were Hebe and your own
Great son. Then the haze lifted to disclose

A young fellow with husky biceps, and,
Like a true hero, Iolaus caught
The king's own chariot at Sciron's rocks.   860
He's brought that chief who used to be so high
And mighty back with him, a prisoner
Of war with hands tied up. The lesson of
The thing is very plain. Don't envy men
Because they seem to have a run of luck,   865
Since luck's a nine days' wonder. Wait their end.

Chorus

Give thanks to Zeus, who fought for us. At last
A day on which our worries are removed.

Alcmene

Hail Zeus! You took your time in helping me,
But I'm not less obliged to you for that.   870
And now I know my son is really with
The gods, although I had my doubts before.
Children, just think! You're safe from danger now!
Safe from the king, who's going to die like
A dog. You'll soon set eyes upon your own   875
Country and have the soil that's yours by right
Beneath your feet. At last you'll worship those
Gods of your fathers who were banned for you
While you were poor and homeless. Tell me, though,
Why didn't Iolaus kill the king?   880
What's back of it? To me there is no point
In being kind to captured enemies.

Attendant

But it was done for you, so you could see
Eurystheus in his glory, in our hands.
It was brute force that brought him in, and not   885
His own accord, since he'd no heart to see
Your face, or pay the price for what he'd done.
And now goodbye. Please don't forget what you
First said when I began, that you would set
Me free; since I should think it's best to keep   890

Faith in these things. *Noblesse oblige*, you know.

(*Exit Attendant.*)

Chorus

STROPHE

There's nothing like the flute's sound when
We dance and sing and eat our fill
And love in all it~ sweetness Then
I feel too glad for words and thrill 895
To see the happy ending for
Those near my heart, in brief, to see
Poor devils had good luck in store
For themselves, thanks to Destiny
And Change and Time. 900

ANTISTROPHE

I hope we keep along the right
Road. Up to now we've paid the high
Gods all their due; it takes a quite
Unbalanced person to deny
It in the face of all the facts, 905
And Zeus himself has verified
It very clearly in his acts
Today, in taking down the pride
Of callous brutes.

STROPHE

Your son, Alcmene, never died. 910
He rules above, and never set
His foot in Hades, or inside
The crematory fire, but met
The wedding-god and fell in love
With Hebe, and the two were paid 915
The honors due to children of
Zeus. It was a marriage made
In heaven's gilded halls.

ANTISTROPHE

How small a world it is. They say

159

That Pallas helped the father in   920
The nick of time, and now today
The children's lives have also been
Saved by the goddess' own town.
The pride of that tormentor who
Ill-used them so was taken down,   925
And we'll have nothing more to do
With ruthlessness and greed.

(Enter Attendant with Guards bringing in
Eurystheus in chains.)

Attendant
Madame, we're bringing in, as you can see,
Eurystheus, which must surprise you and
Was the last thing that *he* expected too.   930
He hadn't bargained for this capture at
Your hands, when he set out from home with such
A force, in his insufferable conceit,
To smash this state. But fate arranged affairs
Quite otherwise and turned the tables here.   935
Hyllus and Iolaus, who were at
Work raising a memorial to Zeus,
Told me to bring this man to you and make
You happy, since there's nothing like the sight
Of an old enemy down on his luck.   940

Alcmene
You brute! So God has punished you at last.
Come, turn this way! Or haven't you the nerve?
To look your enemies straight in the eye?
By God, you'll take the orders that you used
To give us, if you really are the man   945
Who piled humiliations upon my
Poor son. You filthy scum! You made him go
To hell before he died; you sent him out
To kill off hydras, lions, not to speak
Of all the other horrors—it would take   950
Too long to tell it all. But as though this

Were not enough for you; you drove me and
The children out of temples throughout Greece
Where we had taken refuge, hounding old   955
People and babes in arms until you found
A country that was free and wouldn't scare.
And now you'll get what's coming to you, though
Killing is much too good for you. To pay
For what you've done would take a thousand deaths.   960

Chorus
Wait! You can't put a man to death like that.

Attendant
What was the use of capturing him then?

Alcmene
Show me a law against his being killed!

Chorus
But the authorities won't stand for it.

Alcmene
You mean they don't like killing enemies?   965

Chorus
Not prisoners of war, at any rate.

Alcmene
And Hyllus, too, agreed with that idea?

Chorus
Do you expect him to defy our laws?

Alcmene
Why, then, we should have killed the man at once.

Chorus
That's when the wrong was done, since he's survived. 970

Alcmene
Why, what's the difference? We'll correct it now.

Chorus
No one will lay a hand upon this man.

Alcmene
No one? Suppose I do. Or don't I count?

Chorus
There'll be a strong reaction if you do.

Alcmene
No one can say that I don't love this city,   975
But just let someone try to take away
This man from me, now I've got hold of him.
Call me a reckless fool as often as
You like, and say I don't behave the way
A woman should. I'll kill him all the same.   980

Chorus
We feel for you. God knows that you have cause
Enough to hate this man so terribly.

Eurystheus
Don't think I'm going to grovel to you or
Show the white feather here and beg to save
My skin. In any case, I didn't start   985
This feud of my accord. I knew quite well
That you're my cousin and that Heracles
Was consequently my own flesh and blood.
I couldn't help myself when heaven took
A hand, and Hera saddled me with this   990
Scourge in the first place. Once I had estranged
Your son for good and knew the fight was on,
I racked my brains to make things hard for him
And sat up nights to think of ways to beat
And finish off my enemies, and end   995
The fear that never left me day and night.
I didn't underrate your son and knew
His caliber, to give the man his due
For courage, though he was no friend of mine.
But though he'd died, the others kept alive   1000
The spite. I knew the feud was handed down.
That's why I had to try so hard to get
Them killed or exiled, and to plot and plan;

Those tactics meant the only hope for me.
And in my own place, you'd have beaten off   1005
The snarling cubs left by the lion who
Had hated you. Don't try to tell me that
You'd let them stay at peace, in Argos too.
You missed your chance to kill me at the time
When I was willing, so by all Greek laws   1010
My death pollutes the one who strikes me down.
Athens has let me live and knows enough
To think of piety before revenge.
I rest my case. Remember I was not
Afraid to go, and I'll have blood for blood.   1015
I don't particularly want to die
Or mind it either, and that's how things stand.

Chorus
Take my advice, Alcmene. Let this man
Go, since that's what this city would prefer.

Alcmene
Suppose we kill him—but respect their words?   1020

Chorus
That's fine, but how would you bring that about?

Alcmene
It's simple. All you have to do is let me kill
And let friends call for the body. Far be it
For me to cheat this city of his corpse.
He'll settle his account with me first, though.   1025

Eurystheus
Go on, I won't complain. But since your state
Here wouldn't stoop to kill me, I'll tell you
Of an old oracle of Loxias which
Will help you some day more than you may think.
You'll bury me, just as it stipulates,   1030
Before Athena's own Pallenian shrine,
And as the guest of Athens' soil I'll guard
You and preserve you till the end of time.

But when these children's children march on you
In force, then I'll be their arch-enemy.   1035
That's their idea of thanks, and that's the kind
Of people that you saved. You'll ask why I
Ignored the god and came in the first place.
Because I trusted Hera more and thought
That she'd keep faith. Don't let this woman pour   1040
Libations and blood-offerings on my tomb.
But in revenge I'll spoil the homecoming
Of these, and so my end will do two things
At once; it helps you, and it will hurt these.

Alcmene

What are you waiting for, to put this man   1045
Out of the way, since as you've heard, it makes
Your city safe from us? He's pointed out
Your wisest course, since your worst enemy
Becomes your best friend, once he's underground.
Take him away, and when you've killed him, throw   1050

(*To Guards.*)

Him to the dogs, to scotch his last hope that
He can come back and exile me again.

Chorus

That's the solution. Take away this man.
I want to make sure that our kings are cleared
Of all responsibility in this.   1055

(*Exeunt.*)

HIPPOLYTUS

Translated by David Grene

INTRODUCTION TO *HIPPOLYTUS*

"IF IT is necessary that I say anything about a woman's excellence," says Pericles in the history of Thucydides, "I could sum it up in the words: great is her renown whose name is least upon the lips of men either for good or for ill." This has sometimes been taken as the general view of women in Athenian society of the fifth century B.C. However, we have only to look at the tragic stage to realize that the audience at least was immensely interested in women and in their place in human society. Aristophanes attacks Euripides as the author in whose plays the perverse, violent, or monstrous woman has a leading place, and he cites Medea, Sthenoboea, and Phaedra in support of the justice of his charge. As far as the importance of feminine roles goes, Euripides' two predecessors are as guilty as he is. Clytemnestra, Cassandra, Queen Atossa, Electra, Tecmessa, Antigone, and Deianeira are among the most crucial and carefully worked characters in the plays of Aeschylus and Sophocles.

But it *is* probably true that the Athenian audience noticed with special interest, either with delight or with repulsion, Euripides' gallery of bad women. Medea, Sthenoboea, and Phaedra are the three singled out by Aristophanes. Both Sthenoboea and Phaedra are examples of incestuous love; in the *Hippolytus,* Euripides apparently had to revise an early version of the play in which Phaedra makes her proposal of love direct to her stepson. In the second version the nurse was invented to act as a go-between, and Phaedra's conscious responsibility for the address to Hippolytus is left in doubt. But Phaedra's passion for Hippolytus is still the center of the piece. It is not necessary to debate whether, to the fifth-century Greek, sexual relations between stepmother and stepson would be technically incestuous or not. It is enough that we can be sure that they involved an extreme violation of the trust and affection between father and son, and something worse than that, even if the evil cannot be exactly charted.

The play is framed by a Prologue and an Epilogue, each spoken by a goddess. When these goddesses are identified as Aphrodite and Artemis, it becomes all too easy to allegorize them and see the play as a conflict between Lust and Continence with Phaedra and Hippolytus as the appropriate human representatives. But if this view were correct, surely the point of issue would have to be a conflict where the moral really emerged, where, that is, it was dramatically stated with a fair chance of an outcome in either direction. Hippolytus should be tempted where an ordinary man might fall, and Phaedra yield to a passion which, if blameworthy, is comprehensible. Instead, the monstrousness of the relationship is the hinge on which everything turns. Phaedra, when rejected, must kill herself for shame. Theseus, when he learns of it, is ready to murder his son; Hippolytus, in his defense before his father, says that he is accused of a crime from which even an ordinarily unchaste man would shrink. The truth seems to be that Euripides used a story with an almost Homeric flavor, of rival goddesses and their favorites, to write of the absolute power of passion over the human animal. The more horrible the crime of which she is guilty, the more clear it is that Phaedra is being driven far out of her natural course. The perversity of Hippolytus' ostentatious purity—for so the Greeks certainly regarded it—is the cynical foil to Phaedra's guilty lust. She must fall in love with the one man who is a very monk for continence!

This is certainly the right way to see the play, but the explanation also shows some of the play's weaknesses. The author is deeply concerned with Phaedra—Aristophanes is quite right to see that she is the principal character—and much less with Hippolytus. Consequently, when Phaedra dies, only halfway through the play, Euripides is left to deal with a denouement in which he is only professionally interested, because he must properly tidy up the ends of the story. He does this somewhat mechanically and with a flavor of rhetorical commonplace in the argument between Hippolytus and his father. After the disappearance of Phaedra, he enjoyed himself, one feels, only in writing the messenger's speech, with its exciting account of the young man's death. But the figure of Phaedra and even the nurse's intervention —that dramatist's second thought—and the flimsy ambiguity of motive all remain with us to illustrate what is meant by the statement that Euripides marks the beginning of modern psychological tragedy.

The play was first performed in 428 B.C.

CHARACTERS

Theseus

Hippolytus, his son by the queen of the Amazons

Phaedra, Theseus' wife, stepmother to Hippolytus

A Servant

A Messenger

The Nurse

The Chorus of Palace women, natives of Troezen

A Chorus of huntsmen, in attendance on Hippolytus

The Goddess Aphrodite ⎫ *represent natural forces*
The Goddess Artemis ⎭

HIPPOLYTUS

SCENE: *Troezen, in front of the house of Theseus.*

PROLOGUE

Aphrodite
I am called the Goddess Cypris:
I am mighty among men and they honor me by
    many names.
All those that live and see the light of sun
from Atlas' Pillars to the tide of Pontus
are mine to rule.   5
Such as worship my power in all humility,
I exalt in honor.
But those whose pride is stiff-necked against me
I lay by the heels.
There is joy in the heart of a God also
when honored by men.

Now I will quickly tell you the truth of this story.

Hippolytus, son of Theseus by the Amazon,   10
pupil of holy Pittheus,
alone among the folk of this land of Troezen has
    blasphemed me
counting me vilest of the Gods in Heaven.
He will none of the bed of love nor marriage,
but honors Artemis, Zeus's daughter,   15
counting her greatest of the Gods in Heaven
he is with her continually, this Maiden Goddess, in
    the greenwood.
They hunt with hounds and clear the land of wild
    things,

mortal with immortal in companionship.
I do not grudge him such privileges: why should I?   20
But for his sins against me
I shall punish Hippolytus this day.
I have no need to toil to win my end:
much of the task has been already done.
Once he came from Pittheus' house[1] to the country
   of Pandion
that he might see and be initiate in the holy mysteries.   25
Phaedra saw him
and her heart was filled with the longings of love.
This was my work.
So before ever she came to Troezen
close to the rock of Pallas in view of this land,   30
she dedicated a temple to Cypris.
For her love, too, dwelt in a foreign land.
Ages to come will call this temple after him,
the temple of the Goddess established here.
When Theseus left the land of Cecrops,
flying from the guilty stain of the murder of the
   Pallantids,   35
condemning himself to a year's exile
he sailed with his wife to this land.
Phaedra groans in bitterness of heart
and the goads of love prick her cruelly,
and she is like to die.

---

1. "Pittheus' house": The historian Pausanias, relating the legend of Hippolytus, says: "King Theseus, when he married Phaedra, daughter of the king of Crete, was in a quandary what to do with Hippolytus, his son by his former mistress, Antiope the Amazon. He did not wish that after his own death Hippolytus should rule the children of his legitimate marriage, nor yet that Hippolytus should be ruled by them, for he loved him. So he sent the boy to be brought up by his grandfather Pittheus, who lived in Troezen and ruled there. Theseus hoped that when Pittheus died, Hippolytus might inherit the kingdom, and thus peace within the family be preserved, Hippolytus governing Troezen, and Phaedra's children holding sway in Athens." "Pandion's country" and "land of Cecrops" both signify Attica. Pandion and Cecrops were early legendary heroes of Attica.

But she breathes not a word of her secret and none
  of the servants   40
know of the sickness that afflicts her.
But her love shall not remain thus aimless and
  unknown.
I will reveal the matter to Theseus and all shall
  come out.
Father shall slay son with curses—
this son that is hateful to me.
For once the Lord Poseidon, Ruler of the Sea,
granted this favor to Theseus   45
that three of his prayers to the God should find
  answer.
Renowned shall Phaedra be in her death, but none
  the less
die she must.
Her suffering does not weigh in the scale so much
that I should let my enemies go untouched
escaping payment of that retribution
that honor demands that I have.   50
Look, here is the son of Theseus, Hippolytus!
He has just left his hunting.
I must go away.
See the great crowd that throngs upon his heels
and shouts the praise of Artemis in hymns!   55
He does not know
that the doors of death are open for him,
that he is looking on his last sun.

SCENE I

*(Enter Hippolytus, attended by friends and
servants carrying nets, hunting spears, etc.)*

Hippolytus
Follow me singing
the praises of Artemis,
Heavenly One, Child of Zeus,

Artemis!
We are the wards of your care.   60

      (The Chorus of huntsmen chant.)

Hail, Holy and Gracious!
Hail, Daughter of Zeus!
Hail, Maiden Daughter of Zeus and Leto!   65
Dweller in the spacious sky!
Maid of the Mighty Father!
Maid of the Golden Glistening House!
Hail!
Maiden Goddess most beautiful of all the Heavenly
   Host that lives in Olympus!   70

   *(Hippolytus advances to the altar of Artemis and
          lays a garland on it, praying.)*

My Goddess Mistress, I bring you ready woven
this garland. It was I that plucked and wove it,
plucked it for you in your inviolate Meadow.
No shepherd dares to feed his flock within it: 75
no reaper plies a busy scythe within it:
only the bees in springtime haunt the inviolate
   Meadow.
Its gardener is the spirit Reverence who
refreshes it with water from the river.
Not those who by instruction have profited
to learn, but in whose very soul the seed   80
of Chastity toward all things alike
nature has deeply rooted, they alone
may gather flowers there! the wicked may not.

Loved mistress, here I offer you this coronal;
it is a true worshipper's han that gives it you
to crown the golden glory of your hair.
With no man else I share this privilege
that I am with you and to your words   85
can answer words. True, I may only hear:
I may not see God face to face.

            174

So may I turn the post set at life's end
even as I began the race.

Servant

King—for I will not call you "Master," that belongs
to the Gods only—will you take good advice?

Hippolytus

Certainly I will take good advice. I am not a fool.   90

Servant

In men's communities one rule holds good,
do you know it, King?

Hippolytus

        Not I. What is this rule?

Servant

Men hate the haughty of heart who will not be
the friend of every man.

Hippolytus

        And rightly too:
For haughty heart breeds arrogant demeanor.

Servant

And affability wins favor, then?   95

Hippolytus

Abundant favor. Aye, and profit, too,
at little cost of trouble.

Servant

        Do you think
that it's the same among the Gods in Heaven?

Hippolytus

If we in our world and the Gods in theirs
know the same usages—Yes.

Servant

        Then, King, how comes it

that for a holy Goddess you have not even
a word of salutation?

Hippolytus

Which Goddess?
Be careful, or you will find that tongue of yours   100
may make a serious mistake.

Servant

This Goddess here
who stands before your gates, the Goddess Cypris.

Hippolytus

I worship her—but from a long way off,
for I am chaste.

Servant

Yet she's a holy Goddess,
and fair is her renown throughout the world.

Hippolytus

Men make their choice: one man honors one God,
and one another.

Servant

Well, good fortune guard you!
if you have the mind you should have.   105

Hippolytus

God of nocturnal prowess is not my God.

Servant

The honors of the Gods you must not scant, my son.

Hippolytus

Go, men, into the house and look to supper.
A plentiful table is an excellent thing
after the hunt. And you (*singing out two*) rub down
   my horses.   110
When I have eaten I shall exercise them.
For your Cypris here—a long goodbye to her!

Women describe Phaedra's illness

(The old man is left standing alone on the stage.
He prays before the statue of Aphrodite.)

O Cypris Mistress, we must not imitate
the young men when they have such thoughts
  as these.
As fits a slave to speak, here at your image   115
I bow and worship. You should grant forgiveness
when one that has a young tempestuous heart
speaks foolish words. Seem not to hear them.
You should be wiser than mortals, being Gods.   120

        (Enter Chorus of women, servants in
                    Phaedra's house.)

Chorus
STROPHE
There is a rock streaming with water,
whose source, men say, is Ocean,
and it pours from the heart of its stone a spring
where pitchers may dip and be filled.
My friend was there and in the river water   125
she dipped and washed the royal purple robes,
and spread them on the rock's warm back
where the sunbeams played.
It was from her I heard at first
of the news of my mistress' sorrow.   130

ANTISTROPHE
She lies on her bed within the house,
within the house and fever wracks her
and she hides her golden head in fine-spun robes.
This is the third day   135
she has eaten no bread
and her body is pure and fasting.
For she would willingly bring her life to anchor
at the end of its voyage
the gloomy harbor of death.   140

STROPHE
Is it Pan's frenzy that possesses you

or is Hecate's madness upon you, maid?
Can it be the holy Corybantes,
or the mighty Mother who rules the mountains?
Are you wasted in suffering thus,   145
for a sin against Dictynna, Queen of hunters?
Are you perhaps unhallowed, having offered
no sacrifice to her from taken victims?
For she goes through the waters of the Lake[2]
can travel on dry land beyond the sea,
the eddying salt sea.   150

ANTISTROPHE

Can it be that some other woman's love,
a secret love that hides itself from you,
has beguiled your husband
the son of Erechtheus
our sovereign lord, that prince of noble birth?
Or has some sailor from the shores of Crete   155
put in at this harbor hospitable to sailors,
bearing a message for our queen,
and so because he told her some calamity
her spirit is bound in chains of grief
and she lies on her bed in sorrow?   160

EPODE

Unhappy is the compound of woman's nature;
the torturing misery of helplessness,
the helplessness of childbirth and its madness
are linked to it forever.
My body, too, has felt this thrill of pain,   165
and I called on Artemis, Queen of the Bow;
she has my reverence always
as she goes in the company of the Gods.

But here is the old woman, the queen's nurse   170
here at the door. She is bringing her mistress out.

---

2. Limnae, the Lake, a district in Laconia, was the center of the worship of Artemis in the Peloponnese. From it she is sometimes called Limnaios, or Lady of the Lake.

There is a gathering cloud upon her face.
What is the matter? my soul is eager to know.
What can have made the queen so pale?
What can have wasted her body so?   175

SCENE II

(Enter the Nurse, supporting Phaedra.)

Nurse
A weary thing is sickness and its pains!
What must I do now?
Here is light and air, the brightness of the sky.
I have brought out the couch on which you tossed
in fever—here clear of the house.   180
Your every word has been to bring you out,
but when you're here, you hurry in again.
You find no constant pleasure anywhere
for when your joy is upon you, suddenly
you're foiled and cheated.
There's no content for you in what you have
for you're forever finding something dearer,
some other thing—because you have it not.   185
It's better to be sick than nurse the sick.
Sickness is single trouble for the sufferer:
but nursing means vexation of the mind,
and hard work for the hands besides.
The life of man entire is misery:
he finds no resting place, no haven from calamity.   190
But something other dearer still than life
the darkness hides and mist encompasses;
we are proved luckless lovers of this thing
that glitters in the underworld: no man
can tell us of the stuff of it, expounding   195
what is, and what is not: we know nothing of it.
Idly we drift, on idle stories carried.

Phaedra (to the servants)
Lift me up! Lift my head up! All the muscles
are slack and useless. Here, you, take my hands.

They're beautiful, my hands and arms!   200
Take away this hat! It is too heavy to wear.
Take it away! Let my hair fall free on my shoulders.

Nurse

Quiet, child, quiet! Do not so restlessly
keep tossing to and fro! It's easier
to bear an illness if you have some patience   205
and the spirit of good breeding.
We all must suffer sometimes: we are mortal.

Phaedra

O,
if I could only draw from the dewy spring
a draught of fresh spring water!
If I could only lie beneath the poplars,   210
in the tufted meadow and find my rest there!

Nurse

Child, why do you rave so? There are others here.
Cease tossing out these wild demented words
whose driver is madness.

Phaedra

Bring me to the mountains! I *will* go to the
    mountains!   215
Among the pine trees where the huntsmen's pack
trails spotted stags and hangs upon their heels.
God, how I long to set the hounds on, shouting!
And poise the Thessalian javelin drawing it back—
here where my fair hair hangs above the ear—   220
I would hold in my hand a spear with a steel point.

Nurse

What ails you, child? What is this love of hunting,
and you a lady! Draught of fresh spring water!
Here, beside the tower there is a sloping ridge   225
with springs enough to satisfy your thirst.

Phaedra

Artemis, mistress of the Salty Lake,

mistress of the ring echoing to the racers' hoofs,
if only I could gallop your level stretches,   230
and break Venetian colts!

Nurse
This is sheer madness,
that prompts such whirling, frenzied, senseless words.
Here at one moment you're afire with longing
to hunt wild beasts and you'd go to the hills,
and then again all your desire is horses,
horses on the sands beyond the reach of the breakers.   235
Indeed, it would need to be a mighty prophet
to tell which of the Gods mischievously
jerks you from your true course and thwarts your
    wits!

Phaedra
O, I am miserable! What is this I've done?
Where have I strayed from the highway of good
    sense?   240
I was mad. It was the madness sent from some God
that caused my fall.
I am unhappy, so unhappy! Nurse,
cover my face again. I am ashamed   245
of what I said. Cover me up. The tears
are flowing, and my face is turned to shame.
Rightness of judgment is bitterness to the heart.
Madness is terrible. It is better then
that I should die and know no more of anything.

Nurse
There, now, you are covered up. But my own body   250
when will death cover that? I have learned much
from my long life. The mixing bowl of friendship,
the love of one for the other, must be tempered.
Love must not touch the marrow of the soul.   255
Our affections must be breakable chains that we
can cast them off or tighten them.
That one soul so for two should be in travail

as I for her, that is a heavy burden.   260
The ways of life that are most fanatical
trip us up more, they say, than bring us joy.
They're enemies to health. So I praise less
the extreme than temperance in everything.   265
The wise will bear me out.

Chorus Leader
Old woman, you are Phaedra's faithful nurse.
We can see that she is in trouble but the cause
that ails her is black mystery to us.
We would like to hear you tell us what is the matter.   270

Nurse
I have asked and know no more. She will not tell me.

Chorus Leader
Not even what began it?

Nurse
             And my answer
is still the same: of all this she will not speak.

Chorus Leader
But see how ill she is, and how her body
is wracked and wasted!

Nurse
             Yes, she has eaten nothing
for two days now.   275

Chorus Leader
           Is this the scourge of madness?
Or can it be . . . that death is what she seeks?

Nurse
Aye, death. She is starving herself to death.

Chorus Leader
I wonder that her husband suffers this.

Nurse
She hides her troubles, swears that she isn't sick.

Chorus Leader
But does he not look into her face and see   280
a witness that disproves her?

Nurse
                     No, he is gone.
He is away from home, in foreign lands.

Chorus Leader
Why, you must force her then to find the cause
of this mind-wandering sickness!

Nurse
                     Every means
I have tried and still have won no foot of ground.
But I'll not give up trying, even now.   285
You are here and can in person bear me witness
that I am loyal to my masters always,
even in misfortune's hour.
Dear child, let us both forget our former words.
Be kinder, you: unknit that ugly frown.
For my part I will leave this track of thought: 290
I cannot understand you there. I'll take
another and a better argument.

If you are sick and it is some secret sickness,
here are women standing at your side to help.
But if your troubles may be told to men,   295
speak, that a doctor may pronounce upon it.
So, not a word! Oh, why will you not speak?
There is no remedy in silence, child.
Either I am wrong and then you should correct me:
or right, and you should yield to what I say.
Say something! Look at me!   300

Women, I have tried and tried and all for nothing.
We are as far as ever from our goal.
It was the same before. She was not melted
by anything I said. She would not obey me.

But this you shall know, though to my reasoning
you are more dumbly obstinate than the sea:
If you die, you will be a traitor to your children.   305
They will never know their share in a father's palace.
No, by the Amazon Queen, the mighty rider
who bore a master for your children, one
bastard in birth but true-born son in mind,
you know him well—Hippolytus. . . .
So that has touched you?   310

Phaedra
You have killed me, nurse. For God's sake, I
   entreat you,
never again speak that man's name to me.

Nurse
You see? You have come to your senses, yet despite
   that,
you will not make your children happy nor
save your own life besides.

Phaedra
I love my children.
It is another storm of fate that batters me.   315

Nurse
There is no stain of blood upon your hands?

Phaedra
My hands are clean: the stain is in my heart.

Nurse
The hurt comes from outside? Some enemy?

Phaedra
One I love destroys me. Neither of us wills it.

Nurse
Has Theseus sinned a sin against you then?   320

Phaedra
God keep me equally guiltless in his sight!

Nurse
What is this terror urging you to death?

Phaedra
Leave me to my sins. My sins are not against you.

Nurse
Not of my will, but yours, you cast me off.

Phaedra
Would you force confession, my hand-clasping
  suppliant?   325

Nurse
Your knees too—and my hands will never free you.

Phaedra
Sorrow, nurse, sorrow, you will find my secret.

Nurse
Can I know greater sorrow than losing you?

Phaedra
You will kill me. My honor lies in silence.

Nurse
And then you will hide this honor, though I beseech
  you?   330

Phaedra
Yes, for I seek to win good out of shame.

Nurse
Where honor is, speech will make you more honorable.

Phaedra
O God, let go my hand and go away!

Nurse
No, for you have not given me what you should.

Phaedra
I yield. Your suppliant hand compels my reverence.   335

Nurse
I will say no more. Yours is the word from now.

Phaedra
Unhappy mother, what a love was yours!

Nurse
It is her love for the bull you mean, dear child?

Phaedra
Unhappy sister, bride of Dionysus!

Nurse
Why these ill-boding words about your kin? 340

Phaedra
And I the unlucky third, see how I end!

Nurse
Your words are wounds. Where will your tale conclude?

Phaedra
Mine is an inherited curse. It is not new.

Nurse
I have not yet heard what I most want to know.

Phaedra
If you could say for me what I must say for myself. 345

Nurse
I am no prophet to know your hidden secrets.

Phaedra
What is this thing, this love, of which they speak?

Nurse
Sweetest and bitterest, both in one, at once.

Phaedra
One of the two, the bitterness, I've known.

Nurse
Are you in love, my child? And who is he? 350

Phaedra
There is a man, . . . his mother was an Amazon. . . .

Nurse
You mean Hippolytus?

Phaedra
                         You
have spoken it, not I.

Nurse
What do you mean? This is my death.
Women, this is past bearing. I'll not bear
life after this. A curse upon the daylight!
A curse upon this shining sun above us!   355
I'll throw myself from a cliff, throw myself headlong!
I'll be rid of life somehow, I'll die somehow!
Farewell to all of you! This is the end for me.

The chaste, they love not vice of their own will,
but yet they love it. Cypris, you are no God.
You are something stronger than God if that can be.   360
You have ruined her and me and all this house.

> (*The Nurse goes off. The Chorus forms
> into two half-choruses.*)

First Half-chorus
Did you hear, did you hear
the queen crying aloud,
telling of a calamity
which no ear should hear?

Second Half-chorus
I would rather die
than think such thoughts as hers.   365

First Half-chorus
I am sorry for her trouble.

Second Half-chorus
Alas for troubles, man-besetting.

First Half-chorus (*turning to Phaedra*)
You are dead, you yourself
have dragged your ruin to the light.
What can happen now in the long
dragging stretch of the rest of your days?
Some new thing will befall the house.   370

Chorus (*united*)
We know now, we know now
how your love will end,
poor unhappy Cretan girl!

Phaedra
Hear me, you women of Troezen who live
in this extremity of land, this anteroom to Argos.
Many a time in night's long empty spaces   375
I have pondered on the causes of a life's shipwreck.
I think that our lives are worse than the mind's
    quality
would warrant. There are many who know virtue.
We know the good, we apprehend it clearly.   380
But we can't bring it to achievement. Some
are betrayed by their own laziness, and others
value some other pleasure above virtue.
There are many pleasures in a woman's life—
long gossiping talks and leisure, that sweet curse.
Then there is shame that thwarts us. Shame is of
    two kinds.   385
The one is harmless, but the other a plague.
For clarity's sake, we should not talk of "shame,"
a single word for two quite different things.
These then are my thoughts. Nothing can now seduce
    me   390
to the opposite opinion. I will tell you
in my own case the track which my mind followed.
At first when love had struck me, I reflected
how best to bear it. Silence was my first plan.
Silence and concealment. For the tongue
is not to be trusted: it can criticize   395

another's faults, but on its own possessor
it brings a thousand troubles.
Then I believed that I could conquer love,
conquer it with discretion and good sense.
And when that too failed me, I resolved to die.   400
And death is the best plan of them all. Let none
 of you
dispute that.
It would always be my choice
to have my virtues known and honored. So
when I do wrong I could not endure to see
a circle of condemning witnesses.
I know what I have done: I know the scandal: 405
and all too well I know that I am a woman,
object of hate to all. Destruction light
upon the wife who herself plays the tempter
and strains her loyalty to her husband's bed
by dalliance with strangers. In the wives   410
of noble houses first this taint begins:
when wickedness approves itself to those
of noble birth, it will surely be approved
by their inferiors. Truly, too, I hate
lip-worshippers of chastity who own
a lecherous daring when they have privacy.
O Cypris, Sea-Born Goddess, how can they   415
look frankly in the faces of their husbands
and never shiver with fear lest their accomplice,
the darkness, and the rafters of the house
take voice and cry aloud?
This then, my friends, is my destruction:
I cannot bear that I should be discovered   420
a traitor to my husband and my children.
God grant them rich and glorious life in Athens—
famous Athens—freedom in word and deed,
and from their mother an honorable name.
It makes the stoutest-hearted man a slave
if in his soul he knows his parents' shame.   425

The proverb runs: "There is one thing alone
that stands the brunt of life throughout its course,
a quiet conscience," . . . a just and quiet conscience
whoever can attain it.
Time holds a mirror, as for a young girl,
and sometimes as occasion falls, he shows us
the ugly rogues of the world. I would not wish
that I should be seen among them.   430

Chorus Leader
How virtue is held lovely everywhere,
and harvests a good name among mankind!

                         (*The Nurse returns.*)

Nurse
Mistress, the trouble you have lately told me,
coming on me so suddenly, frightened me;
but now I realize that I was foolish.   435
In this world second thoughts, it seems, are best.
Your case is not so extraordinary,
beyond thought or reason. The Goddess in her anger
has smitten you, and you are in love. What wonder
is this? There are many thousands suffer with you.
So, you will die for love! And all the others,   440
who love, and who will love, must they die, too?
How will that profit them? The tide of love,
at its full surge, is not withstandable.
Upon the yielding spirit she comes gently,
but to the proud and the fanatic heart   445
she is a torturer with the brand of shame.
She wings her way through the air; she is in the sea,
in its foaming billows; from her everything,
that is, is born. For she engenders us
and sows the seed of desire whereof we're born,   450
all we her children, living on the earth.
He who has read the writings of the ancients
and has lived much in books, he knows
that Zeus once loved the lovely Semele;

he knows that Dawn, the bright light of the world,
once ravished Cephalus hence to the God's company   455
for love's sake. Yet all these dwell in heaven.
They are content, I am sure, to be subdued
by the stroke of love.
But you, you won't submit! Why, you should certainly
have had your father beget you on fixed terms   460
or with other Gods for masters, if you don't like
the laws that rule this world. Tell me, how many
of the wise ones of the earth do you suppose
see with averted eyes their wives turned faithless;
how many erring sons have fathers helped
with secret loves? It is the wise man's part   465
to leave in darkness everything that is ugly.

Nurse is not very moral

We should not in the conduct of our lives
be too exacting. Look, see this roof here—
these overarching beams that span your house—
could builders with all their skill lay them dead
    straight?
You've fallen into the great sea of love
and with your puny swimming would escape!   470
If in the sum you have more good luck than ill,
count yourself fortunate—for you are mortal.

Come, dear, give up your discontented mood.
Give up your railing. It's only insolent pride
to wish to be superior to the Gods.   475
Endure your love. The Gods have willed it so.
You are sick. Then try to find some subtle means
to turn your sickness into health again.
There are magic love charms, spells of enchantment;
we'll find some remedy for your love-sickness.
Men would take long to hunt devices out,   480
if we the women did not find them first.

Chorus Leader
Phaedra, indeed she speaks more usefully
for today's troubles. But it is you I praise.

And yet my praise brings with it more discomfort
than her words: it is bitterer to the ear.   485

Phaedra
This is the deadly thing which devastates
well-ordered cities and the homes of men—
that's it, this art of oversubtle words.
It's not the words ringing delight in the ear
that one should speak, but those that have the power
to save their hearer's honorable name.

Nurse
This is high moralizing! What you want   490
is not fine words, but the man! Come, let's be done.
And tell your story frankly and directly.
For if there were no danger to your life,
as now there is—or if you could be prudent,
I never would have led you on so far,   495
merely to please your fancy or your lust.
But now a great prize hangs on our endeavors,
and that's the saving of a life—yours, Phaedra,
there's none can blame us for our actions now.

Phaedra
What you say is wicked, wicked! Hold your tongue!
I will not hear such shameful words again.

Nurse
O, they are shameful! But they are better than   500
your noble-sounding moral sentiments.
"The deed" is better if it saves your life:
than your "good name" in which you die exulting.

Phaedra
For God's sake, do not press me any further!
What you say is true, but terrible!
My very soul is subdued by my love
and if you plead the cause of wrong so well   505
I shall fall into the abyss
from which I now am flying.

Nurse
If that is what you think, you should be virtuous.
But if you are not, obey me: that is next best.
It has just come to my mind, I have at home   510
some magic love charms. They will end your trouble;
they'll neither harm your honor nor your mind.
They'll end your trouble, . . . only you must be brave.   515

Phaedra
Is this a poison ointment or a drink?

Nurse
I don't know. Don't be overanxious, child,
to find out what it is. Accept its benefits.

Phaedra
I am afraid of you: I am afraid
that you will be too clever for my good.

Nurse
You are afraid of everything. What is it?

Phaedra
You surely will not tell this to Hippolytus?   520

Nurse
Come, let that be: I will arrange all well.
Only, my lady Cypris of the Sea,
be my helper you. The other plans I have
I'll tell to those we love within the house;
that will suffice.

(*The Nurse goes off.*)

Chorus

STROPHE

Love distills desire upon the eyes,   525
love brings bewitching grace into the heart
of those he would destroy.
I pray that love may never come to me
with murderous intent,
in rhythms measureless and wild.

Not fire nor stars have stronger bolts 530
than those of Aphrodite sent
by the hand of Eros, Zeus's child.

ANTISTROPHE

In vain by Alpheus' stream, 535
in vain in the halls of Phoebus' Pythian shrine
the land of Greece increases sacrifice.
But Love the King of Men they honor not, 540
although he keeps the keys
of the temple of desire,
although he goes destroying through the world,
author of dread calamities
and ruin when he enters human hearts.

STROPHE

The Oechalian maiden who had never known 545
the bed of love, known neither man nor marriage,
the Goddess Cypris gave to Heracles.
She took her from the home of Eurytus,
maiden unhappy in her marriage song,
wild as a Naiad or a Bacchanal, 550
with blood and fire, a murderous hymenaeal!

ANTISTROPHE

O holy walls of Thebes and Dirce's fountain 555
bear witness you, to Love's grim journeying:
once you saw Love bring Semele to bed,
lull her to sleep, clasped in the arms of Death,
pregnant with Dionysus by the thunder king. 560
Love is like a flitting bee in the world's garden
and for its flowers, destruction is in his breath.

SCENE III

*(Phaedra is standing listening near the
central door of the palace.)*

Phaedra
Women, be silent!

(She listens and then recoils.)

Oh, I am destroyed forever.   565

Chorus Leader
What is there terrible within the house?

Phaedra
Hush, let me hear the voices within!

Chorus Leader
And I obey. But this is sorrow's prelude.

Phaedra (cries out)
Oh, I am the most miserable of women!   570

*(The Chorus Leader and the Chorus babble
excitedly among themselves.)*

What does she mean by her cries?
Why does she scream?
Tell us the fear-winged word, Mistress, the fear-
winged word,
rushing upon the heart.

Phaedra
I am lost. Go, women, stand and listen there
yourselves   575
and hear the tumult that falls on the house.

Chorus Leader
Mistress, you stand at the door.
It is you who can tell us best
what happens within the house.   580

Phaedra
Only the son of the horse-loving Amazon,
Hippolytus, cursing a servant maid.

Chorus Leader
My ears can catch a sound,   585
but I can hear nothing clear.

I can only hear a voice
scolding in anger.

Phaedra
It is plain enough. He cries aloud against
the mischievous bawd who betrays her mistress' love.   590

Chorus Leader
Lady, you are betrayed!
How can I help you?
What is hidden is revealed.
You are destroyed.
Those you love have betrayed you.

Phaedra
She loved me and she told him of my troubles,
and so has ruined me. She was my doctor,
but her cure has made my illness mortal now.

Chorus Leader
What will you do? There is no cure.

Phaedra
I know of one, and only one—quick death.
That is the only cure for my disease.   600

> (*She retires into the palace through one of the
> side doors just as Hippolytus issues through the
> central door, dogged by the Nurse. Phaedra is
> conceived of as listening from behind her door
> during the entire conversation between the
> Nurse and Hippolytus.*)

Hippolytus
O Mother Earth! O Sun and open sky!
What words I have heard from this accursed tongue!

Nurse
Hush, son! Someone may hear you.

Hippolytus
You cannot
expect that I hear horror and stay silent.

Nurse
I beg of you, entreat you by your right hand,
your strong right hand, . . . don't speak of this!   605

Hippolytus
Don't lay your hand on me! Let go my cloak!

Nurse
By your knees then, . . . don't destroy me!

Hippolytus
                                        What is this?
Don't you declare that you have done nothing wrong?

Nurse
Yes, but the story, son, is not for everyone.

Hippolytus
Why not? A pleasant tale makes pleasanter telling,
when there are many listeners.   610

Nurse
You will not break your oath to me, surely you
    will not?

Hippolytus
My tongue swore, but my mind was still unpledged.

Nurse
Son, what would you do?
You'll not destroy your friends?

Hippolytus
                        "Friends" you say!
I spit the word away. None of the wicked
are friends of mine.

Nurse
                    Then pardon, son. It's natural
that we should sin, being human.   615

Hippolytus
Women! This coin which men find counterfeit!

Why, why, Lord Zeus, did you put them in the world,
in the light of the sun? If you were so determined
to breed the race of man, the source of it
should not have been women. Men might have
   dedicated
in your own temples images of gold,   620
silver, or weight of bronze, and thus have bought
the seed of progeny, . . . to each been given
his worth in sons according to the assessment
of his gift's value. So we might have lived
in houses free of the taint of women's presence.
But now, to bring this plague into our homes   625
we drain the fortunes of our homes. In this
we have a proof how great a curse is woman.
For the father who begets her, rears her up,
must add a dowry gift to pack her off
to another's house and thus be rid of the load.
And he again that takes the cursed creature   630
rejoices and enriches his heart's jewel
with dear adornment, beauty heaped on vileness.
With lovely clothes the poor wretch tricks her out
spending the wealth that underprops his house.   635
That husband has the easiest life whose wife
is a mere nothingness, a simple fool,
uselessly sitting by the fireside.
I hate a clever woman—God forbid   640
that I should ever have a wife at home
with more than woman's wits! Lust breeds mischief
in the clever ones. The limits of their minds
deny the stupid lecherous delights.
We should not suffer servants to approach them,   645
but give them as companions voiceless beasts,
dumb, . . . but with teeth, that they might not
   converse,
and hear another voice in answer.
But now at home the mistress plots the mischief,
and the maid carries it abroad. So you, vile woman,   650
came here to me to bargain and to traffic

in the sanctity of my father's marriage bed.
I'll go to a running stream and pour its waters
into my ear to purge away the filth.
Shall I who cannot even hear such impurity,
and feel myself untouched, . . . shall I turn sinner?   655
Woman, know this. It is my piety saves you.
Had you not caught me off my guard and bound
my lips with an oath, by heaven I would not refrain
from telling this to my father.
Now I will go and leave this house until
Theseus returns from his foreign wanderings,
and I'll be silent. But I'll watch you close.   660
I'll walk with my father step by step and see
how you look at him, . . . you and your mistress both.
I have tasted of the daring of your infamy.
I'll know it for the future. Curses on you!
I'll hate you women, hate and hate and hate you,
and never have enough of hating. . . .
                                            Some
say that I talk of this eternally,   665
yes, but eternal, too, is woman's wickedness.
Either let someone teach them to be chaste,
or suffer me to trample on them forever.

(*Phaedra comes out from behind the door.*
Exit Hippolytus.)

Phaedra
Bitter indeed is woman's destiny!
I have failed. What trick is there now, what cunning
    plea   670
to loose the knot around my neck?
I have had justice. O earth and the sunlight!
Where shall I escape from my fate?
How shall I hide my trouble?
What God or man would appear
to bear hand or part in my crime?   675
There is a limit to all suffering and I have reached it.
I am the unhappiest of women.

199

Chorus
Alas, mistress, all is over now   680
your servant's schemes have failed and you are
  ruined.

(Enter the Nurse.)

Phaedra
This is fine service you have rendered me,
corrupted, damned seducer of your friends!
May Zeus, the father of my fathers' line,
blot you out utterly, raze you from the world
with thunderbolts! Did I not see your purpose,   685
did I not say to you, "Breathe not a word of this"
which now overwhelms me with shame? But you,
you did not hold back. And therefore I must die
and die dishonored.
Enough of this. We have a new theme now.
The anger of Hippolytus is whetted.
He will tell his father all the story of your sin   690
to my disparagement. He will tell old Pittheus, too.
He will fill all the land with my dishonor.
May my curse
light upon you, on you and all the others
who eagerly help unwilling friends to ruin.

Nurse
Mistress, you may well blame my ill-success,   695
for sorrow's bite is master of your judgment.
But I have an answer to make if you will listen.
I reared you up. I am your loyal servant.
I sought a remedy for your love's sickness,
and found, . . . not what I sought
Had I succeeded, I had been a wise one.   700
Our wisdom varies in proportion to
our failure or achievement.

Phaedra
                    So, that's enough

for me? Do I have justice if you deal me
my death blow and then say "I was wrong: I grant it."

Nurse
We talk too long. True I was not wise then.
But even from this desperate plight, my child,   705
you can escape.

Phaedra
    You, speak no more to me.
You have given me dishonorable advice.
What you have tried has brought dishonor too.
Away with you!
Think of yourself. For me and my concerns
I will arrange all well.

       (Exit Nurse.)

You noble ladies of Troezen, grant me this,   710
this one request, that what you have heard here
you wrap in silence.

Chorus Leader
I swear by holy Artemis, child of Zeus,
never to bring your troubles to the daylight.

Phaedra
I thank you. I have found one single blessing   715
in this unhappy business, one alone,
that I can pass on to my children after me
life with an uncontaminated name,
and myself profit by the present throw
of Fortune's dice. For I will never shame you,
my Cretan home, nor will I go to face   720
Theseus, defendant on an ugly charge,
never—for one life's sake.

Chorus Leader
What is the desperate deed you mean to do,
the deed past cure?

Phaedra

Death. But the way of it, that
is what I now must plan.

Chorus Leader

Oh, do not speak of it!

Phaedra

No, I'll not speak of it. But on this day
when I shake off the burden of this life   725
I shall delight the Goddess who destroys me,
the Goddess Cypris.
Bitter will have been the love that conquers me,
but in my death I shall at least bring sorrow,
upon another, too, that his high heart
may know no arrogant joy at my life's shipwreck;
he will have his share in this my mortal sickness   730
and learn of chastity in moderation.

Chorus

STROPHE

Would that I were under the cliffs, in the secret
    hiding-places of the rocks,
that Zeus might change me to a winged bird
and set me among the feathered flocks.
I would rise and fly to where the sea   735
washes the Adriatic coast,
and to the waters of Eridanus.
Into that deep-blue tide,
where their father, the Sun, goes down,
the unhappy maidens weep
tears from their amber-gleaming eyes   740
in pity for Phaethon.

ANTISTROPHE

I would win my way to the coast,
apple-bearing Hesperian coast,
of which the minstrels sing.
Where the Lord of the Ocean
denies the voyager further sailing,   745

202

and fixes the solemn limit of Heaven
which Giant Atlas upholds.
There the streams flow with ambrosia
by Zeus's bed of love,
and holy earth, the giver of life,   750
yields to the Gods rich blessedness.

STROPHE

O Cretan ship with the white sails,
from a happy home you brought her,
my mistress over the tossing foam, over the salty sea,   755
to bless her with a marriage unblest.
Black was the omen that sped her here,
black was the omen for both her lands,
for glorious Athens and her Cretan home,
as they bound to Munychia's pier   760
the cables' ends with their twisted strands
and stepped ashore on the continent.

ANTISTROPHE

The presage of the omen was true;   765
Aphrodite has broken her spirit
with the terrible sickness of impious love.
The waves of destruction are over her head,
from the roof of her room with its marriage bed,
she is tying the twisted noose.   770
And now it is around her fair white neck!
The shame of her cruel fate has conquered.
She has chosen good name rather than life:
she is easing her heart of its bitter load of love.   775

Nurse (within)
Ho, there, help!
You who are near the palace, help!
My mistress, Theseus' wife, has hanged herself.

Chorus Leader
It is done, she is hanged in the dangling rope.
Our Queen is dead.

Nurse (within)
Quick! Someone bring a knife! 780
Help me cut the knot around her neck.

(*The Chorus talks among itself.*)

First Woman
What shall we do, friends? Shall we cross the
    threshold,
and take the Queen from the grip of the tight-drawn
    cords?

Second Woman
Why should we? There are servants enough within
for that. Where hands are overbusy,
there is no safety. 785

Nurse (within)
Lay her out straight, poor lady.
Bitter shall my lord find her housekeeping.

Third Woman
From what I hear, the queen is dead.
They are already laying out the corpse.

SCENE IV

(*Theseus enters.*)

Theseus
Women, what is this crying in the house? 790
I heard heavy wailing on the wind,
as it were servants, mourning. And my house
deigns me no kindly welcome, though I come
crowned with good luck from Delphi.
The doors are shut against me. Can it be
something has happened to my father? He is old. 795
His life has traveled a great journey,
but bitter would be his passing from our house.

Chorus Leader
King, it is not the old who claim your sorrow.
Young is the dead and bitterly you'll grieve.

Theseus
My children . . . has death snatched a life away?

Chorus Leader
Your children live—but sorrowfully, King.   800
Their mother is dead.

Theseus
         It cannot be true, it cannot.
My wife! How could she be dead?

Chorus Leader
She herself tied the rope around her neck.

Theseus
Was it grief and numbing loneliness drove her to it,
or has there been some violence at work?

Chorus Leader
I know no more than this. I, too, came lately
to mourn for you and yours, King Theseus.   805

Theseus
Oh,
Why did I plait this coronal of leaves,
and crown my head with garlands, I the envoy
who find my journey end in misery.

(To the servants within.)

Open the doors! Unbar the fastenings,
that I may see this bitter sight, my wife
who killed me in her own death.   810

*(The doors are opened, and Theseus goes inside.
The Chorus in the Orchestra divide again
into half-choruses and chant.)*

205

First Half-chorus
Woman unhappy, tortured,
your suffering, your death,
has shaken this house to its foundations.

Second Half-chorus
You were daring, you who died
in violence and guilt.
Here was a wrestling: your own hand against your
    life.   815

Chorus (united)
Who can have cast a shadow on your life?

SCENE V

(Enter Theseus.)

Theseus
O city, city! Bitterness of sorrow!
Extremest sorrow that a man can suffer!
Fate, you have ground me and my house to dust,
fate in the form of some ineffable
pollution, some grim spirit of revenge.   820
The file has whittled away my life until
it is a life no more.
I am like a swimmer that falls into a great sea:
I cannot cross this towering wave I see before me.   825

My wife! I cannot think
of anything said or done to drive you to this horrible
    death.
You are like a bird that has vanished out of my hand.
You have made a quick leap out of my arms
into the land of Death.
It must be the sin of some of my ancestors in the
    dim past   830
God in his vengeance makes me pay now.

Chorus Leader
You are not the only one, King.

Many another as well as you
has lost a noble wife.   835

Theseus
Darkness beneath the earth, darkness beneath the
   earth!
How good to lie there and be dead,
now that I have lost you, my dearest comrade.
Your death is no less mine.   840
Will any of you
tell me what happened?
Or does the palace keep a flock of you for nothing?

God, the pain I saw in the house!
I cannot speak of it, I cannot bear it.   845
I cannot speak of it, I cannot bear it. I am a dead
   man.
My house is empty and my children orphaned.
You have left them, you
my loving wife—
the best of wives   850
of all the sun looks down on or the blazing stars of
   the night.

Chorus
Woe for the house! Such storms of ill assail it.
My eyes are wells of tears and overrun,
and still I fear the evil that shall come.   855

Theseus
Let her be, let her be:
What is this tablet fastened to her dear hand?
What can she wish to tell me of news?
Have you written begging me to care
for our children or, in entreaty,
about another woman? Sad one, rest confident.   860
There is no woman in the world who shall come to
   this house
and sleep by my side.

Look, the familiar signet ring,
hers who was once my wife!
Come, I will break the seals,
and see what this letter has to tell me.   865

(*The Chorus of women speak singly.*)

First Woman
Surely some God
brings sorrow upon sorrow in succession.

Second Woman
The house of our lords is destroyed: it is no more.   870

Third Woman
God, if it so may be, hear my prayer.
Do not destroy this house utterly. I am a prophet:
I can see the omen of coming trouble.

Theseus
Alas, here is endless sorrow upon sorrow.
It passes speech, passes endurance.   875

Chorus Leader
What is it? Tell us if we may share the story.

Theseus
It cries aloud, this tablet, cries aloud,
and Death is its song!   880

Chorus Leader
Prelude of ruin!

Theseus
I shall no longer hold this secret prisoner
in the gates of my mouth. It is horrible,
yet I will speak.

Citizens,   885
Hippolytus has dared to rape my wife.
He has dishonored God's holy sunlight.

(*He turns in the direction of the sea.*)

Father Poseidon, once you gave to me
three curses. . . . Now with one of these, I pray,
kill my son. Suffer him not to escape,
this very day, if you have promised truly.   890

Chorus Leader
Call back your curses, King, call back your curses.
Else you will realize that you were wrong
another day, too late. I pray you, trust me.

Theseus
I will not. And I now make this addition:
I banish him from this land's boundaries.
So fate shall strike him, one way or the other,
either Poseidon will respect my curse,   895
and send him dead into the House of Hades,
or exiled from this land, a beggar wandering,
on foreign soil, his life shall suck the dregs
of sorrow's cup.

Chorus Leader
Here comes your son, and seasonably, King Theseus.
Give over your deadly anger. You will best   900
determine for the welfare of your house.

(*Enter Hippolytus with companions.*)

Hippolytus
I heard you crying, father, and came quickly.
I know no cause why you should mourn.
Tell me.

(*Suddenly he sees the body of Phaedra.*)

O father, father—Phaedra! Dead! She's dead!   905
I cannot believe it. But a few moments since
I left her. . . . And she is still so young.
But what could it be? How did she die, father?
I *must* hear the truth from you. You say nothing
   to me?   910

When you are in trouble is no time for silence.
The heart that would hear everything

is proved most greedy in misfortune's hour.
You should not hide your troubles from your friends,
and, father, those who are closer than your friends.   915

Theseus
What fools men are! You work and work for nothing,
you teach ten thousand tasks to one another,
invent, discover everything. One thing only
you do not know: one thing you never hunt for—
a way to teach fools wisdom.   920

Hippolytus
Clever indeed
would be the teacher able to compel
the stupid to be wise! This is no time
for such fine logic chopping.
                              I am afraid
your tongue runs wild through sorrow.

Theseus
                                    If there were
some token now, some mark to make the division   925
clear between friend and friend, the true and the
    false!
All men should have two voices, one the just voice,
and one as chance would have it. In this way
the treacherous scheming voice would be confuted   930
by the just, and we should never be deceived.

Hippolytus
Some friend has poisoned your ear with slanderous
    tales.
Am I suspected, then, for all my innocence?
I am amazed. I am amazed to hear
your words. They are distraught. They go indeed
far wide of the mark!   935

Theseus
The mind of man—how far will it advance?
Where will its daring impudence find limits?

If human villainy and human life
shall wax in due proportion, if the son
shall always grow in wickedness past his father,
the Gods must add another world to this   940
that all the sinners may have space enough.

Look at this man! He was my son and he
dishonors my wife's bed! By the dead's testimony
he's clearly proved the vilest, falsest wretch.   945
Come—you could stain your conscience with the
  impurity—
show me your face; show it to me, your father.

You are the veritable holy man!
You walked with Gods in chastity immaculate!
I'll not believe your boasts of God's companionship: 950
the Gods are not so simple nor so ignorant.
Go, boast that you eat no meat, that you have Orpheus
for your king. Read until you are demented
your great thick books whose substance is as smoke.
For I have found you out. I tell you all,   955
avoid such men as he. They hunt their prey
with holy-seeming words, but their designs
are black and ugly. "She is dead," you thought,
"and that will save me." Fool, it is chiefly that
which proves your guilt. What oath that you can
  swear,   960
what speech that you can make for your acquittal,
outweighs this letter of hers? You'll say, to be sure,
she was your enemy and that the bastard son
is always hateful to the legitimate line.
Your words would argue her a foolish merchant
whose stock of merchandise was her own life
if she should throw away what she held dearest
to gratify her enmity for you.   965

Or you will tell me that this frantic folly
is inborn in a woman's nature; man
is different: but I know that young men

are no more to be trusted than a woman
when love disturbs the youthful blood in them.
The very male in them will make them false.   970
But why should I debate against you in words?
Here is the dead, surest of witnesses.
Get from this land with all the speed you can
to exile—may you rot there! Never again
come to our city, God-built Athens, nor
to countries over which my spear is king.   975

If I should take this injury at your hands
and pardon you, then Sinis of the Isthmus,
whom once I killed, would vow I never killed him,
but only bragged of the deed. And Sciron's rocks
washed by the sea would call me liar when
I swore I was a terror to ill-doers.   980

Chorus Leader
I cannot say of any man: he is happy.
See here how former happiness lies uprooted!

Hippolytus
Your mind and intellect are subtle, father:
here you have a subject dressed in eloquent words;
but if you lay the matter bare of words,   985
the matter is not eloquent. I am
no man to speak with vapid, precious skill
before a mob, although among my equals
and in a narrow circle I am held
not unaccomplished in the eloquent art.
That is as it should be. The demagogue
who charms a crowd is scorned by cultured experts.
But here in this necessity I must speak.   990
First I shall take the argument you first
urged as so irrefutable and deadly.
You see the earth and air about you, father?
In all of that there lives no man more chaste
than I, though you deny it.   995
It is my rule to honor the Gods first

and then to have as friends only such men
as do no sin, nor offer wicked service,
nor will consent to sin to serve a friend
as a return for kindness. I am no railer
at my companions. Those who are my friends   1000
find me as much their friends when they are absent
as when we are together.

There is one thing that I have never done, the thing
of which you think that you convict me, father,
I am a virgin to this very day.
Save what I have heard or what I have seen in
    pictures,   1005
I'm ignorant of the deed. Nor do I wish
to see such things, for I've a maiden soul.
But say you disbelieve my chastity.
Then tell me how it was *your* wife seduced me:
was it because she was more beautiful
than all the other women in the world?   1010
Or did I think, when I had taken her,
to win your place and kingdom for a dowry
and live in your own house? I would have been
a fool, a senseless fool, if I had dreamed it.
Was rule so sweet? Never, I tell you, Theseus,
for the wise. A man whom power has so enchanted
must be demented. I would wish to be   1015
first in the contests of the Greeks,
but in the city I'd take second place
and an enduring happy life among
the best society who are my friends.
So one has time to work, and danger's absence
has charms above the royal diadem.   1020
But a word more and my defense is finished.
If I had one more witness to my character,
if I were tried when *she* still saw the light,
deeds would have helped you as you scanned your
    friends
to know the true from the false. But now I swear,

I swear to you by Zeus, the God of oaths,   1025
by this deep-rooted fundament of earth,
I never sinned against you with your wife
nor would have wished or thought of it.
If I have been a villain, may I die
unfamed, unknown, a homeless stateless beggar,
an exile! May the earth and sea refuse   1030
to give my body rest when I am dead!
Whether your wife took her own life because
she was afraid, I do not know. I may not speak
further than this.
Virtuous she was in deed, although not virtuous:
I that have virtue used it to my ruin.   1035

Chorus Leader
You have rebutted the charge enough by your oath:
it is a great pledge you took in the God's name.

Theseus
Why, here's a spell-binding magician for you!
He wrongs his father and then trusts his craft,
his smooth beguiling craft to lull my anger.   1040

Hippolytus
Father, I must wonder at this in you.
If I were father now, and you were son,
I would not have banished you to exile! I
would have killed you if I thought you touched my
    wife.

Theseus
This speech is worthy of you: but you'll not die so.   1045
A quick death is the easiest of ends
for miserable men. No, you'll go wandering
far from your fatherland and beg your way.
This is the payment of the impious man.   1050

Hippolytus
What will you do? You will not wait until

214

time's pointing finger proves me innocent.
Must I go at once to banishment?

Theseus

                   Yes, and had I the power,
your place of banishment would be beyond
the limits of the world, the encircling sea
and the Atlantic Pillars.
That is the measure of my hate, my son.

Hippolytus

Pledges, oaths, and oracles—you will not test them?   1055
You will banish me from the kingdom without trial?

Theseus

This letter here is proof without lot-casting.
The ominous birds may fly above my head:
they do not trouble me.

Hippolytus

                Eternal Gods!
Dare I speak out, since I am ruined now   1060
through loyalty to the oath I took by you?
No, he would not believe who should believe
and I should be false to my oath for nothing.

Theseus

This is more of your holy juggling!
I cannot stomach it. Away with you!
Get from this country—and go quickly!   1065

Hippolytus

Where shall I turn? What friend will take me in,
when I am banished on a charge like this?

Theseus

Doubtless some man who loves to entertain
his wife's seducers welcoming them at the hearth.

Hippolytus

That blow went home.   1070
I am near crying when I think that I

am judged to be guilty and that it is you who are
   judge.

Theseus
You might have sobbed and snivelled long ago,
and thought of that before when you resolved
to rape your father's wife.

Hippolytus
             House, speak for me!
Take voice and bear me witness if I have sinned.   1075

Theseus
You have a clever trick of citing witnesses,
whose testimony is dumb. Here is your handiwork.

                  (*Points to the body.*)

It, too, can't speak—but it convicts you.

Hippolytus
If I could only find
another *me* to look me in the face
and see my tears and all that I am suffering!

Theseus
Yes, in self-worship you are certainly practiced.   1080
You are more at home there than in the other virtues,
justice, for instance, and duty toward a father.

Hippolytus
Unhappy mother mine, and bitter birth-pangs,
when you gave me to the world! I would not wish
on any of my friends a bastard's birth.

Theseus (*to the servants*)
Drag him away!
Did you not hear me, men, a long time since
proclaiming his decree of banishment?   1085

Hippolytus
Let one of them touch me at his peril! But you,
you drive me out yourself—if you have the heart!

Theseus
I'll do it, too, unless you go at once.
No, there is no chance that pity for your exile
will steal on my hard heart and make me change.

(*Theseus goes out.*)

Hippolytus
So, I'm condemned and there is no release.   1090
I know the truth and dare not tell the truth.

(*He turns to the statue of Artemis.*)

Daughter of Leto, dearest of the Gods to me,
comrade and partner in the hunt, behold me,
banished from famous Athens.
Farewell, city! Farewell Erechtheus' land!   1095
Troezen, farewell! So many happy times
you knew to give a young man, growing up.
This is the last time I shall look upon you,
the last time I shall greet you.

(*To his companions.*)

Come friends, you are of my age and of this country,
say your farewells and set me on my way.
You will not see a man more innocent—   1100
innocent despite my judge!—condemned to banishment.

(*Hippolytus goes out.*)

Chorus

STROPHE
The care of God for us is a great thing,
if a man believe it at heart:
it plucks the burden of sorrow from him.
So I have a secret hope   1105
of someone, a God, who is wise and plans;
but my hopes grow dim when I see
the deeds of men and their destinies.

For fortune is ever veering, and the currents of life
  are shifting
shifting, wandering forever.   1110

ANTISTROPHE

This is the lot in life I seek
and I pray that God may grant it me,
luck and prosperity
and a heart untroubled by anguish.
And a mind that is neither false clipped coin,
nor too clear-eyed in sincerity,   1115
that I may lightly change my ways,
my ways of today when tomorrow comes,
and so be happy all my life long.

STROPHE

My heart is no longer clear: 1120
I have seen what I never dreamed,
I have seen the brightest star of Athens,
stricken by a father's wrath,
banished to an alien land.   1125

Sands of the seashore!
Thicket of the mountain!
Where with his pacing hounds
he hunted wild beasts and killed
to the honor of holy Dictynna.   1130

ANTISTROPHE

He will never again mount his car
with its span of Venetian mares,
nor fill the ring of Limnae with the sound of horses'
  hoofs.
The music which never slept
on the strings of his lyre, shall be dumb,   1135
shall be dumb in his father's house.
The haunts of the Goddess Maid
in the deep rich meadow shall want their crowns.
You are banished: there's an end   1140
of the rivalry of maids for your love.

Epode

But my sorrow shall not die,
still my eyes shall be wet with tears
for your heartless doom.
Sad mother, you bore him in vain: 1145
I am angry against the Gods.
Sister Graces, why did you let him go
guiltless, out of his native land,
out of his father's house?   1150

But here I see Hippolytus' servant,
in haste making for the house, his face sorrowful.

Scene VI

(Enter a Messenger.)

Messenger
Where shall I go to find King Theseus, women?
If you know, tell me. Is he within doors?   1155

Chorus
Here he is coming out.

Messenger
King Theseus,
I bring you news worthy of much thought
for you and all the citizens who live
in Athens' walls and boundaries of Troezen.

Theseus
What is it? Has some still newer disaster   1160
seized my two neighboring cities?

Messenger
Hippolytus is dead: I may almost say dead:
he sees the light of day still, though the balance
that holds him in this world is slight indeed.

Theseus
Who killed him? I can guess that someone hated him,
whose wife he raped, as he did mine, his father's.   1165

EURIPIDES

Messenger
It was the horses of his own car that killed him,
they, and the curses of your lips,
the curses you invoked against your son,
and prayed the Lord of Ocean to fulfill them.

Theseus
O Gods—Poseidon, you are then truly
my father! You have heard my prayers.   1170
How did he die? Tell me. How did the beam
of Justice's dead-fall strike him, my dishonorer?

Messenger
We were combing our horses' coats beside the sea,
where the waves came crashing to the shore. And we
    were crying
for one had come and told us that our master,   1175
Hippolytus, should walk this land no more,
since you had laid hard banishment upon him.
Then he came himself down to the shore to us,
with the same refrain of tears,
and with him walked a countless company
of friends and young men his own age.   1180

But at last he gave over crying and said:
Why do I rave like this? It is my father
who has commanded and I must obey him.
Prepare my horses, men, and harness them.
There is no longer a city of mine.
Then every man made haste. Before you could say
    the words,   1185
there was the chariot ready before our master.
He put his feet into the driver's rings,
and took the reins from the rail into his hands.
But first he folded his hands like this and prayed: 1190
Zeus, let me die now, if I have been guilty!
Let my father know that he has done me wrong,
whether I live to see the day or not.

220

With that, he took the goad and touched the horses.
And we his servants followed our master's car,   1195
close by the horses' heads, on the straight road
that leads to Argos and to Epidaurus.
When we were entering the lonely country
the other side of the border, where the shore   1200
goes down to the Saronic Gulf, a rumbling
deep in the earth, terrible to hear,
growled like the thunder of Father Zeus.
The horses raised their heads, pricked up their ears,
and gusty fear was on us all to know,
whence came the sound. As we looked toward the
      shore,   1205
where the waves were beating, we saw a wave appear,
a miracle wave, lifting its crest to the sky,
so high that Sciron's coast was blotted out
from my eye's vision. And it hid the Isthmus
and the Asclepius Rock. To the shore it came,   1210
swelling, boiling, crashing, casting its surf around,
to where the chariot stood.
But at the very moment when it broke,
the wave threw up a monstrous savage bull.
Its bellowing filled the land, and the land echoed it,   1215
with shuddering emphasis. And sudden panic
fell on the horses in the car. But the master—
he was used to horses' ways—all his life long
he had been with horses—took a firm grip of the
      reins   1220
and lashed the ends behind his back and pulled
like a sailor at the oar. The horses bolted:
their teeth were clenched upon the fire-forged bit.
They heeded neither the driver's hand nor harness
nor the jointed car. As often as he would turn them   1225
with guiding hand to the soft sand of the shore,
the bull appeared in front to head them off,
maddening the team with terror.
But when in frenzy they charged toward the cliffs,   1230

the bull came galloping beside the rail,
silently following until he brought disaster,
capsizing the car, striking the wheel on a rock.
Then all was in confusion. Axles of wheels,
and lynch-pins flew up into the air,   1235
and he the unlucky driver, tangled in the reins,
was dragged along in an inextricable
knot, and his dear head pounded on the rocks,
his body bruised. He cried aloud and terrible
his voice rang in our ears: Stand, horses, stand!   1240
You were fed in my stables. Do not kill me!
My father's curse! His curse! Will none of you
save me? I am innocent. Save me!

Many of us had will enough, but all
were left behind in the race. Getting free of the reins,
somehow he fell. There was still life in him.   1245
But the horses vanished and that ill-omened monster,
somewhere, I know not where, in the rough cliffs.

I am only a slave in your household, King Theseus,
but I shall never be able to believe   1250
that your son was guilty, not though the tribe of
  women
were hanged for it, not though the weight of tablets
of a high pine of Ida, filled with writing,
accused him—for I know that he was good.

Chorus Leader
It has been fulfilled, this bitter, new disaster,   1255
for what is doomed and fated there is no quittance.

Theseus
For hatred of the sufferer I was glad
at what you told me. Still, he was my son.
As such I have reverence for him and the Gods:
I neither rejoice nor sorrow at this thing.   1260

Messenger
What is your pleasure that we do with him?

Would you have him brought to you? If I might counsel,
you would not be harsh with your son—now he is unfortunate.

Theseus
Bring him to me that I may see his face.   1265
He swore that he had never wronged my wife.
I will refute him with God's punishing stroke.

Chorus
Cypris, you guide men's hearts
and the inflexible
hearts of the Gods and with you
comes Love with the flashing wings,   1270
comes Love with the swiftest of wings.
Over the earth he flies
and the loud-echoing salt-sea.
He bewitches and maddens the heart
of the victim he swoops upon.   1275
He bewitches the race of the mountain-hunting
lions and beasts of the sea,
and all the creatures that earth feeds,
and the blazing sun sees—
and man, too—
over all you hold kingly power,   1280
Love, you are only ruler
over all these.

Epilogue

Artemis
I call on the noble king, the son of Aegeus,
to hear me! It is I, Artemis, child of Leto.   1285

Miserable man, what joy have you in this?
You have murdered a son, you have broken nature's laws.
Dark indeed was the conclusion

you drew from your wife's lying accusations,
but plain for all to see is the destruction
to which they led you.
There is a hell beneath the earth: haste to it,   1290
and hide your head there! Or will you take wings,
and choosing the life of a bird instead of man
keep your feet from destruction's path in which they
    tread?
Among good men, at least, you have no share in life.   1295
Hear me tell you, Theseus, how these things came
    to pass.
I shall not better them, but I will give you pain.
I have come here for this—to show you that your
    son's heart
was always just, so just that for his good name
he endured to die. I will show you, too,
the frenzied love that seized your wife, or I may call it,   1300
a noble innocence. For that most hated Goddess,
hated by all of us whose joy is virginity,
drove her with love's sharp prickings to desire
your son. She tried to overcome her love
with the mind's power, but at last against her will,
she fell by the nurse's stratagems,   1305
the nurse, who told your son under oath her mistress
    loved him.
But he, just man, did not fall in with her
counsels, and even when reviled by you
refused to break the oath he had pledged.
Such was his piety. But your wife fearing
lest she be proved the sinner wrote a letter,   1310
a letter full of lies; and so she killed
your son by treachery; but she convinced you.

Theseus
Alas!

Artemis
This is a bitter story, Theseus. Stay,

hear more that you may groan the more.
You know you had three curses from your father,   1315
three, clear for you to use? One you have launched,
vile wretch, at your own son, when you might have
spent it upon an enemy. Your father,
King of the Sea, in loving kindness to you
gave you, by his bequest, all that he ought.
But you've been proved at fault both in his eyes   1320
and mine in that you did not stay for oaths
nor voice of oracles, nor gave a thought
to what time might have shown; only too quickly
you hurled the curses at your son and killed him.

Theseus
Mistress, I am destroyed.

Artemis
You have sinned indeed, but yet you may win pardon.   1325
For it was Cypris managed the thing this way
to gratify her anger against Hippolytus.
This is the settled custom of the Gods:
No one may fly in the face of another's wish:
we remain aloof and neutral. Else, I assure you,   1330
had I not feared Zeus, I never would have endured
such shame as this—my best friend among men
killed, and I could do nothing.
As for you, in the first place ignorance acquits you,
and then your wife, by her death, destroyed the proofs,   1335
the verbal proofs which might have still convinced
    you.
You and I are the chief sufferers, Theseus.
Misfortune for you, grief for me.
The Gods do not rejoice when pious worshippers die: 1340
the wicked we destroy, children, house and all.

Chorus
Here comes the suffering Hippolytus,
his fair young body and his golden head,
a battered wreck. O trouble of the house,

what double sorrow from the hand of God   1345
has been fulfilled for this our royal palace!

Hippolytus
A battered wreck of body! Unjust father,
and oracle unjust—this is your work.
Woe for my fate!   1350
My head is filled with shooting agony,
and in my brain there is a leaping fire.
Let me be!
For I would rest my weary frame awhile.
Curse on my team! How often have I fed you   1355
from my own hand, you who have murdered me!
O, O!
In God's name touch my wounded body gently.
Who is this standing on the right of me?   1360
Come lift me carefully, bear me easily,
a man unlucky, cursed by my own father
in bitter error. Zeus, do you see this,
see me that worshipped God in piety,   1365
me that excelled all men in chastity,
see me now go to death which gapes before me;
all my life lost, and all for nothing now
labors of piety in the face of men?

O the pain, the pain that comes upon me!   1370
Let me be, let me be, you wretches!
May death the healer come for me at last!
You kill me ten times over with this pain.
O for a spear with a keen cutting edge   1375
to shear me apart—and give me my last sleep!
Father, your deadly curse!
This evil comes from some manslaying of old,   1380
some ancient tale of murder among my kin.
But why should it strike me, who am clear of guilt?
What is there to say? How can I shake from me   1385
this pitiless pain? O death, black night of death,
resistless death, come to me now the miserable,
and give me sleep!

Artemis
Unhappy boy! You are yoked to a cruel fate.
The nobility of your soul has proved your ruin.   1390

Hippolytus
O divine fragrance! Even in my pain
I sense it, and the suffering is lightened.
The Goddess Artemis is near this place.

Artemis
She is, the dearest of the Gods to you.

Hippolytus
You see my suffering, mistress?   1395

Artemis
I see it. Heavenly law forbids my tears.

Hippolytus
Gone is your huntsman, gone your servant now.

Artemis
Yes, truly: but you die beloved by me.

Hippolytus
Gone is your groom, gone your shrine's guardian.

Artemis
Cypris, the worker of mischief, so contrived.   1400

Hippolytus
Alas, I know the Goddess who destroyed me!

Artemis
She blamed your disrespect, hated your chastity.

Hippolytus
She claimed us three as victims then, did Cypris?

Artemis
Your father, you, and me to make a third.

Hippolytus
Yes, I am sorry for my father's suffering.   1405

Artemis
Cypris deceived him by her cunning snares.

Hippolytus
O father, this is sorrow for you indeed!

Theseus
I, too, am dead now. I have no more joy in life.

Hippolytus
I sorrow for you in this more than myself.

Theseus
Would that it was I who was dying instead of you!   1410

Hippolytus
Bitter were Poseidon's gifts, my father, bitter.

Theseus
Would that they had never come into my mouth.

Hippolytus
Even without them, you would have killed me—
you were so angry.

Theseus
          A God tripped up my judgment.

Hippolytus
O, if only men might be a curse to Gods!   1415

Artemis
Hush, that is enough! You shall not be unavenged,
Cypris shall find the angry shafts she hurled
against you for your piety and innocence
shall cost her dear.
I'll wait until she loves a mortal next time,   1420
and with this hand—with these unerring arrows
I'll punish him.

To you, unfortunate Hippolytus,
by way of compensation for these ills,
I will give the greatest honors of Troezen.

Unwedded maids before the day of marriage   1425
will cut their hair in your honor. You will reap
through the long cycle of time, a rich reward in tears.
And when young girls sing songs, they will not forget
    you,
your name will not be left unmentioned,
nor Phaedra's love for you remain unsung.   1430

                        (*To Theseus.*)

Son of old Aegeus, take your son
to your embrace. Draw him to you. Unknowing
you killed him. It is natural for men
to err when they are blinded by the Gods.

                        (*To Hippolytus.*)

Do not bear a grudge against your father.   1435
It was fate that you should die so.
Farewell, I must not look upon the dead.
My eye must not be polluted by the last
gaspings for breath. I see you are near this.

Hippolytus
Farewell to you, too holy maiden! Go in peace.   1440
You can lightly leave a long companionship.
You bid me end my quarrel with my father,
and I obey. In the past, too, I obeyed you.

The darkness is upon my eyes already.

Father, lay hold on me and lift me up.   1445

Theseus
Alas, what are you doing to me, my son?

Hippolytus
I am dying. I can see the gates of death.

Theseus
And so you leave me, my hands stained with murder.

Hippolytus
No, for I free you from all guilt in this.

Theseus
You will acquit me of blood guiltiness?   1450

Hippolytus
So help me Artemis of the conquering bow!

Theseus
Dear son, how noble you have proved to me!

Hippolytus
Yes, pray to heaven for such legitimate sons.

Theseus
Woe for your goodness, piety, and virtue.

Hippolytus
Farewell to you, too, father, a long farewell!   1455

Theseus
Dear son, bear up. Do not forsake me.

Hippolytus
This is the end of what I have to bear.
I'm gone. Cover my face up quickly.

Theseus
Pallas Athene's famous city,
what a man you have lost! Alas for me!   1460
Cypris, how many of your injuries
I shall remember.

Chorus
This is a common grief for all the city;
it came unlooked for. There shall be
a storm of multitudinous tears for this;
the lamentable stories of great men   1465
prevail more than of humble folk.